Message In The Night

by

David Turner

Flame Publishing

2

Contents:

4

Introduction

"But God chose the foolish things of the world to shame the wise; God chose the weak things of the world to shame the strong. He chose the lowly things of this world and the despised things and the things that are not to nullify the things that are so that no one may boast before Him." (1 Corinthians 1:27-29)

I would have to say a big "Amen" to this verse because foolish, weak, lowly, and despised are exactly from where the Lord has brought me! I was as lost as a duck in the middle of the desert! By His great mercy and kindness, God has lifted me from the wreckage of a ruined and messed up life.

One day, as I was going to sing a song I had written, the pastor of my church began to introduce me by saying, "Not long ago, as this young man drove by with his long hair flopping everywhere and looking so wild and weird, I stopped and wondered if a person like that could ever be saved."

God certainly works in strange and mysterious ways. It is strange that He would save a person like me, whom no one thought would ever be saved. But not only has the Lord saved me, He has called and appointed me to do a very important work for His kingdom. It is amazing to realize that some of the most important things in the Bible were accomplished by God using people whom no one would have ever thought He would have used. For some reason, I don't think He has changed His style!

One night, the Lord came in a powerful and awesome way and spoke a message to me. The main purpose in writing this book is to deliver this message and to say all that God has called me to say concerning this message. I hope and pray that it will help you find His pathway that leads to the eternal "Promised Land."

Chapter 1

From a Frog to a Prince

If you were passing through the small town of Mountain Grove, Missouri in the year 1970, you might have caught a glimpse of a strange sight. Back then, there weren't many of us long-haired guys around that part of the country. Most folks just called us "hippies."

One day I had my long hair pulled back in a ponytail, and as I passed some older ladies on the sidewalk I heard them whisper, "Did you see that? Oh my, isn't that just a sight!"

I had my own farm out in the country then, where I grew things. I did grow quite a lot of "plants" to smoke one year, mostly on my neighbors' property (I figured it would be better if they got busted instead of me!)

Thank God, His arm of mercy is not short. It can reach people who are "way out there," and that's exactly what happened to me!

One day, by His wonderful kindness and mercy, God reached down and touched me. When the Lord came into my life, it was like a light shining in the midst of total darkness. It was a light that led me away from the dangerous road of destruction I had been traveling on for several years. It was a light that led me to find the way of hope, the way of help, and the way of life — Jesus, my Savior.

My dad died when I was very young, and by the time I was a teenager, the yardstick my mom used to spank me just didn't seem to scare me much anymore. I guess that's why I decided I could get away with smoking.

I hid my cigarettes under the seat of my motorcycle to keep my smoking a secret from my mother. But one day I looked back after taking off really fast on my motorcycle and noticed that I had left a long trail of cigarettes all across the yard. I was hurrying to pick them all up when my mom came out and told me she had known for a long time that I'd been smoking. Much to my surprise, she told me she also knew I'd been drinking.

"David," she said, "I always know the minute you walk in the door when you've been drinking. Usually, you just kind of flop around when you walk, but when you come home after you've been drinking, you try and walk straight and stiff as a board." I guess the only one I was fooling was myself.

My drinking habits caused me a lot of problems back in those days. I lost my license twice when I was arrested for driving while intoxicated. I was often thrown into jail for public drunkenness and disturbing the peace. I was in several drinking-related car wrecks, which placed me in a high risk of totally destroying myself.

By the time I was a senior in high school, my smoking and drinking had taken the edge off my athletic abilities, so I dropped out of all sports. My bad habits continued in college where I majored in parties and minored in girls — or maybe it was the other way around. I guess it doesn't really matter, since I only went for one year.

I quit college when I decided to buy a farm near where I grew up. I had lived and worked on a farm my whole life, so this seemed to be a good move. It was around this time that an old school friend introduced me to smoking pot. I was nervous BIG TIME about doing this, but he assured me he had been smoking the stuff for a long time and it was no big deal. So I tried it...and was hooked!

I had always wanted to let my hair grow out, but every time I tried, I always had to cut it off for one reason or another. But now the cows on my farm didn't seem to mind, so I just let my hair grow until it was about two-thirds of the way to my waist. By this time, I guess I had become a genuine, full-blown hippie! I'm not quite sure what that means, but it was what most folks in those parts called me and a handful of other guys who had long hair at that time.

My philosophy consisted of trying to turn every day into some kind of wild party — smoking pot, doing drugs, drinking, or all the above. By the time I was 22 years old, my life was a wreck, and I had grown tired of the whole scene. It wasn't like it was a "new thing" anymore. It seemed like for every ounce of fun I was having, a hundred pounds of problems came along! I was searching to find some meaning and purpose in life, but only ending up empty-handed and frustrated — totally confused about myself and the world. All I had was a bunch of questions and no answers. Seeing some of my close friends die, and others completely destroy their lives because of their involvement with drugs and alcohol made me really start worrying about how I might end up. I could see that my life was falling apart. I had messed up most of my friendships by doing things while I was drunk or stoned that made people just want to stay away from me. More and more I felt frustrated, confused, and depressed.

It seemed like I was trapped inside of a life that I didn't even like any more, but I couldn't see any way to change or get out of it. Can you imagine taking a piece of uncooked spaghetti and bending it slowly until you feel like it's going to snap? That's the way I felt. I had pushed my mind and body so hard I felt like something on the inside was just going to break — something that couldn't be fixed.

One day my oldest brother came to me and gave me a little money. He told me everyone in the family was deeply concerned about me.

"You just don't look good, Dave," he said. "We're all worried that if you keep going in the direction you're going, you might not be around too much longer."

I guess I was so frustrated that somewhere along the way, I had stopped caring much about life. When you get to that place, you take greater risks, and life's road becomes dangerous to travel.

Fortunately, it was about this time something good did happen — I met a girl named Pam, and we started dating. I still don't know how or why, but she actually started liking me.

It was great when we were together, but she sure made me a nervous wreck when she would talk about us getting married. Man, I couldn't take care of myself, let alone anyone else. Thoughts of the big "M" were really scary! You know, that's the big permanent thing that you're supposed to do right — but I wasn't doing anything right! I figured I'd blow the whole thing just like I'd been blowing everything else in my life. My relationship with Pam was the greatest thing that had ever happened to me, but it made me really worry because something inside was telling me I wasn't going to ever be able to tell this girl good-bye.

One day, while I was at Pam's apartment waiting for her to get ready for our date, I picked up a small piece of paper I saw lying on a table and started to read it. It was a Gospel tract someone had left on her door that day. It talked about how a person couldn't find any real happiness in things like money, drugs, booze, sex, etc., but that the only way to find real and lasting happiness is in accepting Jesus as your Savior.

It also said that when people accept Jesus as Savior, all their sins are forgiven, and they receive eternal life.

I slipped the tract into my pocket and read it again later that night. I started to think a lot about what it said. I sure wasn't happy the way I was. I thought if only all this "Jesus stuff" was real, maybe I could be happy!

Now all of this didn't exactly make me want to run out and start going to church, but it definitely got me interested in checking out the Bible. I felt like a great magnet was drawing me as I turned to the Bible and started searching for truth and reality, hoping to find some better way.

I started picking up the Bible whenever and wherever I could and reading a little bit from one book and then another. Then one day I decided to read the whole thing through. I was intensely searching for some kind of proof that what the Bible says has happened has really happened — some kind of existing evidence I could see in the world today.

It was important for me to see something real in the Bible upon which to base my faith because I grew up knowing many people who went to church every Sunday, but their walk with God was totally phony. I knew make-believe religion was not going to help me. My situation was desperate, and I needed something totally real!

I started in Genesis and read how God created the whole world, how He made the sun and moon and all the stars, how He made the plants and animals, and how He created Adam and Eve. I was really trying to believe all of that and have faith, but I must admit, it seemed pretty far out there.

Then, when I started reading about Noah and the Ark, I just about lost it! Man, I really wanted to believe, but the story about this Noah dude seemed to push me way out somewhere into cartoon-land. I remember thinking, *Wow, if I keep reading stuff like this, I'll never need drugs again!*

But then I began to read about a man named Abraham. It was here that I found what I had been searching for — something the Bible says has happened that there is solid, concrete proof actually existing in the world today showing clearly that it has really happened. What I found in the very first book of the Bible was so important that it became one of the main foundation blocks of my faith.

Beginning in Chapter twelve of Genesis, the Bible tells of a great promise God made about four thousand years ago to a man named Abraham. God promised to greatly bless the numbers of Abraham's descendants so that they would become a nation. He also gave to Abraham a specific piece of land and promised that his descendants would possess that land <u>forever</u>! Genesis 12:1-2 reads: *The Lord had said to Abram, "Leave your country, your people and your father's household and go to the land I will show you. I will make you into a great nation and I will bless you; I will make your name great and you will be a blessing."*

When Abraham arrived in this promised land God spoke to him again and said, *"All the land that you see I will give to you and your offspring forever"* (Genesis 13:15). The key word here is "<u>forever</u>."

I knew if this great promise was true, and if God was really real, then this nation that God had promised to Abraham so long ago had to exist somewhere in the world today. And I found it!

The Bible says Abraham had a son named Isaac and then a grandson named Jacob. Genesis 35:10 tells us how God spoke to Jacob and changed his name, *"God said to him, 'Your name is Jacob, but you will no longer be called Jacob; your name will be Israel.' So he named him Israel."* As I read this verse, I experienced the greatest awakening that has ever happened in my life. I began to realize the enormously important truth that the nation of Israel in the world today *is* the nation God promised to Abraham some 4000 years ago — and its name comes from Abraham's grandson "Israel!" It doesn't take rocket science to figure this out, just a little common sense and some child-like faith.

I was amazed as I read the awesome account

of how God created a great nation from this man and his wife who were both far too old to have a child — but did! I had a hard time keeping my mouth from falling open as I read through the amazing account of how the mighty hand of God worked miracle after miracle to bring to pass all He had promised to Abraham.

I remember seeing the movie *The Ten Commandments* when I was a little boy, but I didn't realize that all the great miracles and everything that happened in that movie had actually happened in real life. I had no clue that all of those people Moses led out of the land of Egypt *were* the people of the nation of Israel who were being led to the land God had promised to their "father" Abraham several hundred years earlier!

Seeing how all of this really happened made faith come alive in me. It enabled me to believe that absolutely everything the Bible says is totally true and real — even the incredible story of Noah and the Ark.

My new-found faith gave birth to a sense of amazement and awe. But it also brought overwhelming feelings of fear and guilt. For the first time in my life, I could see that the Mighty God of the Bible is no "Santa Claus." He is for real! And His commandments are not to be taken lightly. As my mind scanned back over the years of my life, my fears increased. I saw clearly that I had broken many of those commandments.

Thoughts of the many warnings Jesus gave us about a place of eternal punishment — a place where people will be tormented by fire forever — terrified me. But then what seemed like a horrifying nightmare became suddenly very real as I realized that I was guilty and condemned before God and actually on my way to this place.

A great sadness and sorrow also filled my heart as I realized how horribly I had treated the One who had freely given me my life — my very existence. I began to realize how much God deserves to be thanked, praised, and worshipped. Life itself comes from Him. He deserves to be everything, but I had made Him nothing. Instead of praising His Holy Name, I had used that name to curse with. Instead of centering my life around pleasing Him as He deserves, I had totally centered it around trying to please myself. And I had made a big mess of the whole thing!

It was really good to have Pam to talk to at that time. She had gone to church a lot and knew much more about the Bible than I did. She was the first person to tell me about Jesus, and how God could forgive me. Her words certainly brought a welcome ray of hope, but the full light of the Gospel just couldn't break through the heavy darkness in my life quite yet. I was overwhelmed by the mountain of sin in my life, and thinking that if God had drawn a "you-can-never-be-forgiven" line out there somewhere, then I had probably crossed it a long time ago. Thank God, there is no such line!

Then came the most important day of my life — a day that happened over two decades ago, but continues to live in my heart and mind as if it were only yesterday. It was the day I found out that the mighty God of the Bible is not only real in the past, He is totally real in the present!

I was doing something that day that was very familiar to me — mowing hay with the tractor in one of our fields. This was a large field that took a long time to drive around, so I had a lot of time to think.

As I thought about my life, I realized I was traveling on a road of destruction that was leading to a dead end. I became totally consumed with sadness and fear. My heart felt broken. I had messed up my life so much and I had treated God horribly. I was overwhelmed with fear as I faced the reality that I was on my way to the place of eternal punishment. I realized there was nothing I could do to help myself out of this situation. As all of this became too much for me, I completely lost control of my emotions. All I could do was lift my face up to the sky and in desperation cry out a three-word prayer: "God help me." I know for sure it wasn't the length of this prayer that got Heaven's attention. But something did! I believe it must have been the heartfelt tears behind those three words.

In only seconds after calling out to God, I began to feel an awesome and glorious power I had never felt before. I could feel it on the inside and all around me.

I didn't know much about God. I don't think at the time I even knew there was such a thing as the Holy Spirit. But what I felt was so strong and so real that although it was too much for me to understand, somehow I knew I was experiencing the presence of God.

I started seeing a very real picture in my mind — kind of like a dream except I was awake. It was like a real-life scene of Jesus suffering and dying on the cross. I knew what I was seeing was coming from this great power I was feeling.

I began to see how Jesus was completely innocent and had done only good things. He did no wrong, so He certainly did not deserve any punishment. Yet he sacrificed His life to die on a cross to take the penalty and punishment of *our* sins upon himself. I was able to see how Jesus has made a way for our sins to be forgiven by taking upon himself the suffering, the pain, and the death that *we* deserve.

For the first time, I began to have hope that there was a way my sins could be forgiven! My heart was deeply touched by what God allowed me to see and understand.

Then something totally incredible happened. God actually spoke to me!

The words I heard were not heard with my human ears; it was as if my whole soul became an ear. These words were very powerful, yet they were full of kindness and compassion.

As God answered my cry for help by revealing to me the most important and precious truth in all the world — the way of forgiveness and salvation that Jesus has made by suffering and dying in our place on the cross — the voice of God spoke to me and said: **"Here is the way that I can help you."**

God's mercy and kindness towards me has been deeper than the ocean and higher than the sky. There's no way I could ever put into adequate words what I saw, felt, and heard that day when I experienced His glory and presence. It changed me forever!

I felt like I needed to do something more. I had watched a few Billy Graham Crusades on TV and saw how people came forward and prayed, so I felt like I should pray and "officially" accept Jesus as my Savior.

However it was a little different for me. There was nobody singing *"Just as I Am,"* and there was no altar where I could pray — I was just in a hay field. But I did find a log that looked like it would work for me, so I knelt down next to it and began to pray.

I prayed to Jesus and told Him I knew I had broken the laws of God and was guilty and facing a very serious penalty. I turned to God with my heart and accepted Jesus as my Savior, believing that His death on the cross had made a way for all my sins to be forgiven. I asked Jesus to come into my life and change me and make me all that He wants me to be.

Since that day, God has inspired me to write many songs that reflect the peace, joy, and hope that replaced the fear, sadness, and guilt in my life.

Do not think you're beyond hope. It doesn't matter how much you have done wrong, for the sacrifice Jesus made on the cross is powerful enough and great enough to take away your sins. Are you a prostitute, an alcoholic, a thief, a drug addict, a murderer? It makes no difference — God still loves you! Jesus died to save you from the penalty of your sins. He has truly opened the gate to life itself for all people who will turn to Him — *no exceptions!*

Are you holding back from turning to God because you feel you can't change your life or live for the Lord? Well, you're right! *You can't* — but *God can* do it for you. He simply wants us to come to Him the way we are and seek forgiveness for our sins. He wants us to accept Jesus as our Savior. Once we do, He will change our lives and empower us to follow Him.

Ever since I turned to God and started following Him, He has blessed me like He blessed Joseph in the Bible. I am a builder/developer now. I turn cow pastures into subdivisions full of houses. God has prospered my business greatly. Nobody would have ever "thunk" that an old hippie dude like me could become so successful!

As I drive through subdivisions our company has developed with streets full of houses we've built, it's hard for me to believe what has happened. That is because it's way bigger than I am. But I know it has happened because somebody far bigger than I am has made it all happen. Money is certainly not the most important thing in life, but I'm glad God has helped me to have money to do some cool things like start this ministry, record my songs, travel to churches, and help other ministries. Thank you God!

I give God the credit and glory for all the great things that has happened in my life including being happily married to a wonderful and beautiful girl named Pam for many years. God has taken the life I had trashed out and has made it greater than any dream I could have ever dreamed — greater than anything I could have ever imagined. And the best is yet to come!

When I realize I am really on my way to Heaven and that when Jesus comes back I'll get to go with Him and live forever, it just makes me want to jump and shout. Man, this is better than winning the world's biggest lottery! I just can't wait to walk on those heavenly streets of gold, to eat the fruit of the Tree of Life, and to see and live forever in God's beautiful city!

Won't it be great to live in a place where there is no sickness or death? No sadness or sorrow? No fighting, no evil, no wrong — a place where everyone will get along in perfect peace and love? The glory of God will shine so brightly, there won't even be any more night!

I know eternity is going to be a long time, but if you're like me, it just won't be long enough to thank and praise our wonderful Creator and to worship Jesus, our Savior and our King!

The thought that God would use someone like myself, a person no one could even imagine ever being saved, to do an important work for His Kingdom is enough to make a person laugh! But God's ways are certainly not man's ways. That must be why Jesus was born in a stable instead of a palace, and why the angels announced His coming to lowly shepherds instead of the "socially and religious elite."

I have traveled to many churches, singing my songs and sharing my testimony for many years. I believe God wants me to continue doing what I have done in the past, but I also believe He wants to expand this ministry to bring a great revival and powerful outpouring of His Spirit among His people. It is the desire of my heart to see God's people turn to Him and seek Him with their whole heart and all of their strength, so they will be empowered by His Spirit to take the life-saving message of Jesus to those who are lost and dying in the world. I believe God has planned to use this ministry to bring a sense of urgency to His people, and lead people to find His narrow pathway that leads to life.

I would like to offer at this time to come to any church or gathering that wants me to come. God has blessed our business in such a great way that I am able to travel and stay as long as God wants me to stay, whether it be one day or several, without asking for any money.

I just want to be totally led by the Spirit of God. As the children of Israel journeyed through the desert, they were led by the Lord. They were instructed to move and follow the cloud of God when it moved from above the tabernacle. I have faith to believe that God has planned to do something awesome through this ministry and that His Spirit will lead the way like it did for the children of Israel. I am glad God has given me songs and music ability in a variety of styles to appeal to different ages and groups of people.

I am giving the contact information below where I can be reached. If you have any questions, you are welcome to contact my office and I will be happy to speak with you.

Flame Ministry
P.O. Box 2501 #254
Springfield, MO. 65801

Telephone: 1-800-864-5289
e-mail: FlameMinistry@aol.com

Chapter 2

A MESSAGE FROM GOD

One evening I was unable to go to sleep because of feeling a great burden for all the people in the world who are lost and on their way to a horrible place of everlasting punishment. I was grieved in realizing that so many of these people are not even aware or concerned about the great danger they are facing because they do not believe in God or the Bible. I thought about Jesus dying on the cross and how He has made a way for these people to go free if they would only turn to Him, and I wondered if I was really doing enough to help them find the way. I decided to get up and pray, and it was during this time of prayer that I experienced a very powerful visitation from God. The word of the Lord came to me saying,

"**The way that many people are trying to come to Me for salvation is not working. Many people's efforts in coming to Me for salvation are as men digging cisterns that hold no water. When people come to Me for salvation, the blood of Jesus must be applied to their hearts. As the blood that was applied to the door frames on the Day of Passover was the only thing that saved the children of Israel from death, it is only as the blood of Jesus is applied to people's hearts today that they are saved from death.**"

God is sending this message to bring awareness of a great "drifting away" from His pathway that leads to real salvation and life.

The Lord is sending a very serious warning along with some very urgently needed guidance through this message and this ministry to all churches and to all people that hope for salvation.

God is saying in the first sentence of this message that there is a very serious problem with the "way" that many people are trying to come to

Him that is causing them to fail in receiving a real salvation experience.

The Amplified Bible says in Psalm 34:18, *"The Lord is close to those who are of a broken heart and saves such as are crushed with sorrow for sin and are humbly and thoroughly penitent."* This verse reveals the acceptable way for us to turn to God for salvation. It shows us that we must humble ourselves before the Lord and have deep sorrow and repentance in our heart for our sins.

The reason many people are failing in their efforts to obtain salvation, as God is warning in this message, is because they are not *first* realizing the seriousness of their sins and the penalty they are facing which leads them to turn to the Lord with real heartfelt repentance. We have all broken the laws of God and have horribly failed to worship Him in the way He deserves. We are all condemned to a place of everlasting punishment that is infinitely more horrible than we could ever imagine because of our sins and failures. This should bring all of us to a place where our hearts are broken and we feel crushed with sorrow because of our sins. However, many people are trying to turn to God in an "easier" or more "comfortable" way by avoiding facing the reality of their sins and guilt before God. Those who turn to God without shedding tears of heartfelt repentance are the ones to whom God is referring in this message and whose efforts end in failure.

In the second sentence of this message God

states, "**Many people's efforts in coming to Me for salvation are as men digging cisterns that hold no water.**"

Back in the days when cisterns were commonly used, people put forth a great amount of effort to make a cistern. The holes had to be dug by hand and then lined with something like brick or stone to keep the collected water clean.

God is saying that many people are spending a lot of time and going to great lengths to obtain salvation but that all their efforts are ending in total failure just like "men digging cisterns that hold no water!"

In the third sentence of this message God makes this infinitely important statement, "**When people come to Me for salvation the Blood of Jesus must be applied to their hearts.**" God is speaking of the great change that *only* happens when His Spirit touches the hearts and transforms the lives of those who turn to Him in an acceptable way. This great "miracle" brings very deep feelings of love and appreciation for Jesus because of the sacrifice He made on the cross by shedding His blood to make a way for our sins to be forgiven. This "divine transformation" is certainly what Jesus was referring to in John 3:7(NIV) when He said, "... You must be born again." It is also what the Apostle Paul was referring to in 2nd Corinthians 5:17(NIV): "Therefore, if anyone is in Christ, he is a new creation, the old has gone, the new has come!"

Through this message, God is warning that many people are failing to receive this "divine transformation" in their hearts and lives because they are not coming to Him in an acceptable way. Most of the preaching in this age lacks the presence of God's power of conviction which leads people to a place of humble repentance. Therefore, multitudes are ending up with a shallow religious experience which only brings a change within their minds, not their hearts.

Each church or denomination has its own ideas of what "procedures" people should go through to be saved. However, what is most important is not the "procedures" but what is in a person's heart when they turn to God for salvation. (1 Samuel 16:7) *"Man looks at the outward appearance, but the Lord looks at the heart."*

Those who fail to humble themselves and turn to God with heartfelt repentance also fail to receive the "touch" from God that changes their hearts and totally transforms their lives. Without this "miracle" from God in their hearts, people never have what it takes on the "inside" to follow the Lord or do the works He has given us to do.

No tears = No miracle = No salvation.

In the last sentence of this message God states, **"As the blood that was applied to the door frames on the Day of Passover was the only thing that saved the children of Israel from death, it is**

only as the blood of Jesus is applied to people's hearts today that they are saved from death."

God is trying to help us get in touch with the urgency of the fact that our position before Him is a matter of life or death!

The last and most horrible plague that God sent upon the land of Egypt was the plague of "death." (Exodus chapter 12) Moses announced that on a certain night all the firstborn in the land of Egypt would die. This plague of death would have come upon the children of Israel had God not provided a way for them to escape what was coming.

God spoke to Moses and instructed him to tell the children of Israel to take the blood of a lamb and place it around the door of their houses, so that when the plague of death passed through the land of Egypt, it would pass over their houses. Thus the children of Israel were saved from "death" by placing the blood of a lamb around their doors.

God has placed the penalty of "death" upon all of us because we have all broken His laws and failed to worship Him as He deserves. We all <u>urgently</u> need to stop and realize how serious this penalty really is because it includes more than the physical death we experience at the end of our life in this world. Hebrews 9:27 states, *"And as it is appointed unto men once to die, but after this the judgment."* This verse tells us that someday all people will be brought back to life and will stand before God in a great day of judgment. Concerning this judgment, Revelation

20:15 says, *"If anyone's name was not found written in the book of life, he was thrown into the lake of fire."* In Revelation 20:14 the Bible says, *"The lake of fire is the second death."* This "second death," is an <u>eternal</u> death!

However, by the greatness of His goodness and mercy God has provided a way for us to escape this horrible penalty of "death" just like He provided a way for the children of Israel to escape the plague of death. God has sent Jesus, "the Lamb of God," into this world to make a way so that we can escape the penalty we <u>all</u> deserve. When Jesus suffered and died on the cross, He took the penalty and punishment of our sins upon Himself and made a way that we can be totally forgiven and set free from the penalty of "death" that has come upon *all* people. By placing the penalty and punishment of our sins upon Jesus, who was perfect and deserved no punishment, God has made a way that we can escape the penalty we deserve if we will turn to Him in faith seeking forgiveness for our sins.

God is saying in this message that we can only be saved when the blood of Jesus is applied to our <u>hearts,</u> as the children of Israel were only saved when they applied the blood of a lamb around their doors. God is saying that our hearts must be touched and changed to receive real salvation. <u>Only</u> the Spirit of God can touch our hearts and apply the blood of Jesus as He is relating in this message, and that is why it is so important to come to the Lord in the way that is acceptable to Him.

Don't Be
Played By The Game

One day I went into a place where video games are played. I walked up to a game I knew how to play called "Galaga." There was a very young boy playing this game, and he was pounding on the buttons and jerking the control stick around and yelling a lot. (When nobody is playing this game the machine will simulate a game being played on the monitor, complete with sound effects and everything.) After I stood there for a couple of minutes, watching this boy frantically going at this game, I realized he wasn't playing the game at all. The machine was merely simulating a game being played. However, it didn't seem to matter to this kid because he was really into it!

Finally, after a long time of watching him "play the game," I said to him, "You know you are not really playing this game don't you?"

He jerked his head away from the video machine only for a split-second, not to interfere with his game, and shouted, "Yes I am, too!"

I walked away after a while, totally amazed that this kid still thought he was really playing that game.

As I walked along, God impressed upon my mind how a lot of people in churches are like this child. They have gone through some religious procedures but have failed to have their hearts and lives touched and changed by the supernatural power of God. They have never really faced the seriousness of their sins and turned to God with their hearts and been really saved. They go to church, but they don't follow the leading of God's Spirit and do the works He has given us to do. They continue to go through religious motions and think they are on the pathway to Heaven, but they are like this boy who never put his quarter in, yet thought he was playing the game.

Reasons For The Failure

I believe God has revealed to me that the main cause of the serious failure that He is warning of in this message is resulting from people's failure to meet and experience the conditions of heartfelt repentance which are necessary for salvation. Many people are failing to humble themselves and are trying to take an "easier way in" by avoiding facing the very unpleasant reality that they have been horribly wrong before God and deserve the punishment that has been placed upon all people. They are being misled to go through procedures of being saved, but because their heart and attitude are not right as they approach God for salvation, they fail to receive the supernatural touch from Him that changes their heart and life. They become "conformed" to man's religion but not "transformed" by the power of God!

I believe God is making known now these areas of serious mistakes which are bringing about this failure:

(1) There is a growing deception in the church that God allows people to come to Him and successfully obtain salvation without humbling themselves to fully realize that they are standing guilty and condemned before Him and deserve the eternal punishment that the Bible states has been placed upon all people.

Many churches and leaders today have adopted the idea that people can turn to God by embracing His love, making a decision to follow Him, or in some easier way, rather than dealing honestly with their sins and guilt before God and turning to Him with deep feelings of repentance. The reason why this trend has become very popular is simply because people would much rather avoid facing the scary reality of their guilty and condemned position before God and not take responsibility for their sins and failures if they are given an "easier" option that they think will work. However, God has His way of doing things and is certainly not obligated to follow along with man's foolish religious "trends." God simply does not allow people to excuse themselves from facing the reality that they are guilty before Him and that the penalty of "death" has been placed upon them. People cannot be released from their guilty and condemned position before God by embracing His love any more than a person who has been convicted of a serious crime can be released by trying to embrace the love of the judge. Salvation requires humble and honest acceptance that we are guilty before God and deserve the penalty of "death" that has been placed upon us.

All people have been separated from the holy presence of God because of our sins. The only way people are allowed to enter again into the presence of God is if they first humble themselves and realize they have sinned and then receive the shed blood of Jesus as an atonement for their sins. The High Priest of Israel could not enter into the presence of God to make the yearly sacrifice for the nation of Israel until he first made an atonement for his own sins, and neither can we today! **The "easier" religious procedures that many people are being offered today as a way to turn to God cannot be substituted in the place of having heartfelt repentance and receiving the blood of Jesus as an atonement for our sins.**

The disastrous result in man following his own way instead of God's way is that God's Spirit is simply not involved in much of what is going on in many churches and ministries today. What churches and ministries *think* has been accomplished through their efforts and what God has actually performed are two very different things. I think it would be good for many church leaders to ask themselves this question: Since salvation is a matter of receiving the shed blood of Jesus as an atonement for our sins, would God really allow the precious blood of His only son to be used as an atonement to cover the sins of any person who is trying to come to Him <u>without</u> having deep feelings of sorrow and guilt for their sins?

Church leaders who continually minimize making people aware of their guilty and condemned position before God and try to lead people to come to God in as easy way as possible may mean well and think they are really helping people. However, the sad truth is that they are actually helping many people to fail because God does not allow anyone to come to Him and successfully obtain salvation by sidestepping or avoiding coming into full awareness of their guilty and condemned position before Him.

Ear-tickling preachers can build churches or ministries that look very successful on the outside. However, large numbers of people and big buildings can be very deceiving. The Tower of Babel was big, but it sure wasn't very successful! Unfortunately, the overall church system has become much like a huge "religious" Tower of Bable because of following man's ways instead of God's way.

(2) Many leaders in the church are giving in to vocational and social pressures which eliminates the flow of the convicting power of God. They preach what people "want" to hear rather than what they urgently "need" to hear. It is obvious that it is extremely unpleasant for anyone to become aware that they are standing guilty and condemned before God and are on their way to a place of eternal punishment because of their sins. It is for this reason that church leaders have increasingly tried to minimize leading people to face the scary reality of how serious their position before God really is. Most leaders are very concerned about the growth and welfare of their church or ministry along with keeping or advancing their position. They fear that people becoming upset and filled with fear because of being made aware of how serious their position before God is will threaten the welfare of their church or ministry or maybe even their job. They therefore minimize dealing with the truth of people's guilty and condemned position before God.

It is a very common human trait for people to have strong tendencies to avoid taking responsibility for their failures and mistakes. Isn't this why Adam and Eve hid from God in the garden after they had disobeyed Him? Unfortunately, this trait makes it easy for many people to take the "easier" pathways to God that are being presented to them by those in positions of leadership. These pathways offer people the opportunity to minimize dealing with the seriousness of their sins and the dangerous penalty that has been placed upon them. People are being deceived into thinking that they can slide comfortably into the Kingdom of God without shedding tears of repentance.

(3) Pride is keeping many people from fully realizing that they are standing guilty and condemned before God and truly deserve eternal punishment. It is the work of the Holy Spirit that enables lost people to see and understand the seriousness of their sins and the fearful and dangerous penalty they are facing. However, many people are resisting and stopping this vital convicting power of God from working in their own lives by refusing to humble themselves before God and accept that they deserve the eternal punishment the Bible states has been placed upon all people.

Many times people who have lived a good or morally disciplined life make the spiritually *fatal* mistake of comparing themselves to others which results in falsely thinking that they are in a more favorable position with God than those who have gone far into sin. However, the Bible does not say anything about God dividing sinners into categories. It just states that we are *all* guilty before God and that the penalty of "death" has come upon <u>all</u> people.

Jesus gave us a great example of this kind of attitude and just how far people get with God who think this way. (Luke 18:9-14) *"Two men went up to the temple to pray, one a Pharisee and the other a tax collector. The Pharisee stood up and prayed about himself: 'God, I thank you that I am not like other men — robbers, evildoers, adulterers — or even like this tax collector. I fast twice a week and give a tenth of all I get.' But the tax collector stood at a distance. He would not even look up to heaven, but beat his breast and said, 'God, have mercy on me, a sinner.' I tell you that this man, rather than the other, went home justified before God. For everyone who exalts himself will be humbled, and he who humbles himself will be exalted."*

I received a letter one day from a woman who had taken great offense in the fact that I proclaim that all people must turn to God fearing the penalty of their sins and with heartfelt repentance. She made this statement, "If you are a person who isn't wallowing in sin, you aren't going to be overwhelmed with the great sin in your life like you were, and so you may not have to have the hell scared out of you. You may need only to embrace God's love for you and desire to know Him more and be like Him."

This person portrays an attitude of pride much like that of the Pharisee mentioned above who thought so highly of himself. I really don't think this lady has ever faced the reality that she is guilty before God and on her way to hell, and I believe that there are a lot of people in the church today that are exactly like her. She makes it clear that she believes that people who have lived a good life do not need to be deeply concerned or filled with fear because of their sins, that somehow these people have obtained a more favorable position with God than those who have committed much sin, and that they deserve to come to God by just embracing his love rather than with tears of repentance.

This woman, and all the people in the world who are like her, have a dangerous overly high opinion of themselves. They may compare themselves to other human beings and think they look pretty good, but the truth is that even the very best of people have been horribly wrong before God. We have all miserably failed to worship God and be as thankful as we should be for the infinitely great gift of "life" that He has given to each one of us. We are all born into this world with a fallen and selfish nature that leads us to break the commandments of God. The truth is that Jesus would still have had to die to save the very best person who has ever lived in this world. Our sins before God are that serious, and they are not to be taken lightly.

I was speaking to a Sunday school teacher one day and was asked the question of how I was saved. I proceeded to tell the person how I became interested and started searching in the Bible after realizing that my life was being ruined and destroyed. I shared that when I became aware that God and everything in the Bible is a reality that I was overwhelmed with great sorrow and fear realizing how wrong I had been towards God and that I was on my way to the place of everlasting punishment. I told this person how I had cried out in desperation to God asking Him to help me and how God then helped me to find and receive the way of help and salvation that Jesus has brought into this world. Then this person turned to me and said, "Well when I came to the Lord I wasn't afraid of going to hell or anything like that, I just wanted to know Him." Unfortunately, the modern church system is filled with many people that are in positions of leadership who are like this Sunday school teacher and have completely failed to become aware of how serious their guilty and condemned position before God really is before approaching the Lord for salvation. They have failed to humble themselves and fully realize that they have broken the laws of God and deserve the penalty of death and hell that has been placed upon all people. They have failed to turn to God in an acceptable way and thus have failed to be touched and changed by God's Spirit . They have become very religious, but are still very lost. Being deceived in thinking they have found the way, they end up misleading many other people to take the same pathway to failure that they have taken.

People who feel like their sins are not serious enough to be deeply concerned about need to quit deceiving themselves and spend some time thinking about what the word "all" really means, and then re-read some very important scriptures like Romans 5:12 KJV, *"Wherefore, as by one man sin entered into the world, and death by sin; and so <u>death</u> passed upon <u>all</u> men, for that <u>all</u> have sinned."*

Many people in the church who feel comfortably saved may not suspect that they have ever had any spiritual pride in their lives. However, people who refuse to humble themselves and accept the fact that they are guilty before God and deserve the eternal punishment the Bible states has been placed upon all people *do* have a very dangerous form of pride in their lives.

It is impossible for any human being to face the reality that they are guilty and condemned before God and are on their way to meet such a horrible punishment and not be totally overwhelmed with fear and sorrow. Only those who refuse to humble themselves before God and face the reality of their sins and the penalty they deserve end up excusing themselves from feeling the fear and sorrow that is appropriate for them to feel because of their sins. Unfortunately, according to the warning that God is sending in this message, they also end up excusing themselves from receiving a real salvation experience from the Lord.

(4) The reason this great failing has spread throughout the entire church system is because many people in positions of leadership in the church have failed *themselves* to receive the spiritual transformation from God that is necessary for real salvation. They therefore lead others down the same pathways to failure that they have experienced, thus duplicating and multiplying the failure that has occurred in their own lives. Blind leading the blind did not occur only when Jesus was here, it is happening on a frightening scale throughout the entire church system of today.

Many people in positions of leadership in the church cannot remember a time in their *own* life when they were overwhelmed with fear and sorrow because of realizing they were guilty and condemned before God and facing the penalty of death and hell. There is no way these leaders can ever lead others to fear the dangerous penalty they face before God because they have never experienced it for themselves! They mislead lost people by making it easy for them to avoid facing the reality of the dangerous penalty they are headed for by leading them down "religiously perfumed" pathways. However, man's religious pathways do not lead to "life," they lead to "death!"

Psalm 127:1, *"Unless the Lord builds the house, its builders labor in vain."*

Show Dogs

When I was a young boy, my brothers and I loved to hunt quail, and we had some very good hunting dogs. These dogs were amazing because they were born with an instinct to point birds. We really did not have to train them to do this. We would usually take them out with an older dog, and they would just naturally hunt due to the ability "born" into them. These dogs had such a great sense of smell. They could smell the birds a long distance away, and then they would freeze like a statue with their heads pointing in the direction of the birds. As you walked toward the birds, the dogs would creep along close to the ground like cats stalking prey.

My cousin, who lived in the city, bought himself two young bird dogs and paid a lot of money for them. They were registered and came from a line of award-winners. He told me if I would train these two dogs he would give one of them to me. I thought this was a great deal because the dogs looked really good. I took them out with an older dog just like we had trained all of our other dogs, but I couldn't get these dogs to do anything right. They acted like they didn't know a bird from a rabbit! I tried everything, but finally had to give up. These dogs were just not "born" with the instinct to hunt. They were not hunting dogs; they were "show" dogs. There was no way a person could ever train them to point birds. They just didn't have what it takes on the inside! I had to finally call my cousin and tell him to come and get the dogs because, as far as hunting dogs go, they were completely worthless!

Many people in the church are a lot like these "show dogs." They look like Christians and talk like Christians. They go to church and go through all the religious procedures, but they do not function like real Christians because they do not have the heart or the spirit of a real Christian on the inside. They do not feel an urgency about the work of God. They do not have a passion that drives them to take the message of Jesus to a lost and dying world. They are not following where the Spirit of God leads because they have never been "born" of the Spirit of God. They do not have what it takes on the inside. They have an outward "show" of religion, but not the presence and power of God on the inside. If people have not been born of the Spirit of God, they will never have real faith and love on the inside, and just like these dogs, no amount of teaching or training will ever make them perform like the real thing!

Statistics gathered by George Barna, Billy Graham Association, and other evangelistic research efforts, reveal that over 95% of people who attend church regularly do not share the urgent message of Jesus with others, and have never led even one person to Christ in their entire life. Jesus tells us in John 14:15, *"If you love me, you will obey what I command."* Then He gives us a command in Mark 16:15: *"Go into all the world and preach the good news to all creation."* The church urgently needs to wake up and realize that a very high percentage of the people they claim to have led to salvation simply do not have enough love and faith in their lives to obey what Jesus has commanded them to do!

By their lack of action to help others find salvation a majority of church members show that they have very little awareness that our position before God is a matter of "life or death." Could their severe lack of awareness and urgency come from never experiencing it for themselves?

When Jesus gave us the Great Commission in Matthew 28:19 (NIV) He said, *"Therefore go and <u>make disciples</u> of all nations, baptizing them in the name of the Father and of the Son and of the Holy Spirit, and teaching them to obey everything I have commanded you."* I think it's time to realize that as far as "making disciples" as Christ has instructed us to do, the church is failing. Disciples are driven by a great love and passion to follow God and take the message of Jesus to the lost world. This love and passion can only come from God, it does not occur naturally. The reason this supernatural love from God that moves people to become disciples is not present in the lives of a very high percentage of church members is because God is not touching the hearts of those who fail to come to Him in humble repentance.

The multitudes of church goers who are not obeying what Jesus has commanded all of us to do have something missing on the inside. That "something" is the love that *only* the Spirit of God can bring when He touches our hearts through salvation. This love is certainly what God is referring to in this message when He says, **"When people come to Me for salvation, the blood of Jesus must be applied to their <u>hearts</u>."**

Whether or not we follow God and make it

to Heaven completely depends on receiving this "touch from God" in our hearts when we turn to Him for salvation. It is the very power that gives us the faith and love to follow Christ and do the works He has given us to do, and without it we are nothing!

There's No Tea In The Cup!

At one of our family gatherings a few years ago one of my little nieces, who was then about four years old, received a miniature toy tea set as a gift. It was a complete set with tiny cups, a tea pot, a little cream pitcher, and sugar bowl all on a nice little serving tray. She brought her tea set to me and asked if I would like some tea. I told her, "Yes, please."

This was the beginning of a little game that went on for over an hour. She pretended to pour me a cup of tea, and then she would ask me if I wanted sugar and then if I wanted cream, and I would always say, "Yes, please" so she could pretend to put sugar and cream in my imaginary cup of tea. This was a cute, harmless game we were playing.

Unfortunately, much of what occurs in the churches of today is a "game" that is not so harmless. People are going through religious motions and procedures without the power or presence of God being involved. Preachers are preaching flowery sermons that do not have the convicting power of God flowing through them. People are trying to come to God for salvation on an intellectual and socially comfortable level instead of coming to Him in fear and sorrow, and with tears of repentance.

Real faith from God has never entered the lives of those who try to come to Him without facing the reality and the seriousness of their sins. People who are not real with God in the beginning end up playing the "church game" of gathering together and pretending to worship. However, the fruitlessness in their lives reveals that this is only a "game" they play on Sunday.

If what goes on in church does not have the power and presence of God in it from the beginning, then the whole thing can become like the little game I played with my niece where we went through the "motions" and "pretended," but there was "**no tea in the cup**."

When the church first started, people mostly met in houses so there was no building with which to be concerned. Leaders did not receive a salary so they didn't have to try to please people in order to keep their jobs. Because of earthly concerns, most leaders today are so obsessed with pleasing people and not disturbing anyone that they have pushed the convicting power of God right out of the church. The result is dead religion! Many churches are not much more than "religious social clubs" filled with people "playing church." They praise God with their lips but have no action of taking the urgent message of Jesus to others which shows that their worship and faith are not real!

Many leaders are making the spiritually fatal mistake of thinking that they can lead people to God some "easier" or more "comfortable" way by preaching about the love and goodness of God and all the blessings of salvation and then getting people to "make a decision." The church has developed several "procedures" that are commonly thought of as ways people can receive salvation. Some of these procedures include asking people to walk forward and: (1) ask Jesus to come into their life, (2) make a decision to follow God, (3) turn their life over to God, (4) give their heart and life to Jesus, (5) make a public profession of their faith, (6) call on the name of the Lord, (7) be baptized and join the church. All of these are good and wonderful things to do and can be a part of salvation. However, they can become very dangerous "*substitutes*" if people are led through these procedures as a way to obtain salvation instead of being led *first* to deal honestly with their sins and guilt before God. People cannot avoid or omit repenting of their sins when they approach God for salvation. Salvation is strictly a matter of receiving the shed blood of Jesus as an atonement for our sins. Unless people come to God honestly and openly dealing with their sins with heartfelt repentance, there is no atonement made! Instead of becoming living and fruitful branches attached to the living vine of God's

Spirit they are misguided to become dead and un-fruitful branches attached to the vine of man's dead religion.

Church leaders who fail to operate in the flow of God's Spirit, are more like spiritual undertakers leading people into dead religion and false hope, than they are like spiritual doctors delivering new babies into the Kingdom of God.

People may think that they are helping others when they tell them that all they have to do is just believe and ask Jesus to come into their lives. However, the church is filled with multitudes of misguided people who have tried to approach God without tears of repentance, and have said or repeated some prescribed religiously shallow prayer. These are the masses of people in the church who have dead faith and no fruit in their lives of helping others find Christ. The zero results in their lives shows that their faith is not real and alive and that there has been no spiritual change in their lives!

God has sacrificed the life of His only son to make a way so our sins can be forgiven. He is certainly not willing to allow anyone to come to Him and receive this holy atonement that was made for their sins unless they first come to a full realization of how serious their sins are and the severe punishment they deserve!

There's Life In The Real Thing

Recently, I was tagging along behind my wife in a store where she was gathering some artificial flowers to make an arrangement. That's something she loves to do and is very good at.

My attention was caught by a display that looked so real I actually had to walk over and touch the flowers to see if they were real or not. Upon touching them, I realized they were artificial, but I stood there thinking how great a job man has done to be able to make these flowers look so real. Then the Spirit of God spoke to me and said, "Man has done a good job of imitating what I have made, but there is no "life" in these flowers. They look real, but there is no life in them."

Then my thoughts were directed to people who go to church and talk about God a lot, but never focus their lives on helping others find Jesus and His way of eternal life. They seem to be like the artificial flowers. They look really good, but because they are made by man's religion and not by God, they have no "life" in them! Jesus said in Matthew 15:13, *"Every plant that my heavenly Father has not planted will be pulled up by the roots."*

Our action, or lack of action, will show whether our faith is real and alive — or as dead as those artificial flowers.

I think it would be a good idea at this time to take a look at some of the things Jesus said and taught.

First of all, Jesus said in Matthew 7:21, *"Not everyone who says to me, Lord, Lord, will enter the kingdom of heaven, but only he who does the <u>will</u> of my Father who is in heaven."* I think the multitudes of people in church who are not obeying the command of Jesus to "go into all the world and preach the Gospel" urgently need to read this verse very carefully. Many people are very involved in "church" but are failing to follow the <u>will</u> of God in *the* very most important area which is taking the message of Jesus to those who are yet lost in the world.

Jesus revealed how great the change is that comes into the lives and hearts of people when they really get saved in the parable of the man who found the hidden treasure in the field (Matthew 13:44). In this parable, when the man found the treasure, he went and sold everything he had so he could buy the field and possess the treasure. Jesus is showing us that when people really get saved, God and His work become everything to them — more important than everything else in the world. Are we supposed to believe that God and His work are everything to those in the church who can't seem to get up off their comfortable church pew and do anything to help others find the way of salvation?

In the parable of the talents (Matthew 25: 14-30), the servant who did nothing with what he had been given was thrown into outer darkness where there is weeping and gnashing of teeth. Considering the severity of this punishment, could Jesus have been referring to anyone else except those who have heard and received the Gospel but done nothing with it? If this is true, then a very high percentage of the people making up the churches of today are in serious trouble because they have accomplished nothing with what they have been given, just like the worthless servant in the parable!

In the parable of the sower (Matthew 13), Jesus shows us that all people who hear the Gospel are separated into four groups. The only good group is like the seeds that fell on good soil that produced a crop of what was sown, which was the message about the Kingdom. The other three groups failed for different reasons. The people making up the churches of today who fall into the category of the groups that failed are doing so because their hearts have not been touched and changed by God's Spirit of love. For example, those who are like the third group that become unfruitful because of being choked by the cares of this life and the pursuit of wealth do so because they have more love for the things of this world than they do for God and His work. Sadly enough, the majority of the people making up the churches of today fall into this failing category.

Jesus said in Matthew 10:37-38, *"Anyone who loves his father or mother more than me is not worthy of me; anyone who loves his son or daughter more than me is not worthy of me; and anyone who does not take his cross and follow me is not worthy of me."* Christ is saying in this verse that in order to be "worthy" of Him, which means worthy to be with Him in His eternal Kingdom, we must have a love for Him that is greater than the love we have for those in our immediate family, a love that we would even be willing to die for. I hope and pray that the multitudes of people in churches of today who do not love Jesus enough to obey His command to take the message of salvation to the lost would be honest with themselves and realize that they do not possess the kind of love that Christ is speaking of in this verse. This love is what God is referring to in the message at the beginning of this chapter when He says, **"The blood of Jesus must be applied to their hearts."** It is a supernatural love that can only come from God. This love is what God is saying many people are failing to receive because they are not turning to Him in a way that is acceptable.

I would like to state very clearly that I am not saying that salvation is earned in any way by our works. The Bible tells us in many places that we are saved by faith. However, no one can be saved with <u>dead</u> faith. James 2:26 says, *"For as the body without the spirit is dead, so faith without works is dead also."* According to James, a person who has no works has dead faith. If there is not enough faith in a person's life to produce any works, then how could there ever have been enough faith in that person's life to produce salvation? The question that people who have no works and dead faith need to ask themselves is, "If my faith is not alive and real enough now to produce works, then was it ever alive and real to begin with?"

The works we do should flow out of a heart of love for God and people. If there are no works then where is that love? Has the heart ever been touched and changed by the Spirit of God?

I am not saying that salvation can be earned in any way by our works, but I am saying that if people have truly been saved then works will naturally flow from their life. The works result from a changed heart that is empowered by the presence of God's Spirit which brings real and living faith and love. If people have no works in their lives, then I believe they should seriously question whether or not God's Spirit has ever been "born" into their lives.

A Parable For Today

Something great always happens when we spend a good amount of time seeking God.

I was staying at a pastor's home in Oregon, and I was praying early on a Sunday morning before I went to sing and speak in his church. As I prayed, the presence of God came in a great way and I received this story.

There was a man who had two young sons. When the boys were small, their father would hold them up and show them an old clock sitting on the fireplace mantle. He would always tell the boys they could never touch the clock because it belonged to his grandfather and was very valuable to him.

One day the father went to town and while he was gone the boys decided if they were very careful, they could get the clock down and play with it. Then they heard the door open and their father say, "Boys, I'm home!" In their excitement, they dropped the clock and broke it.

The father was very angry and disappointed because the old clock meant a lot to him. So he told the boys they must come to him and say they were sorry or they would be punished. One of the sons did not have a good attitude and he really wasn't sorry, but he didn't want to get punished so he approached his father and said in a not-so-serious tone, "Well, I guess I'm sorry."

The other boy was truly sad because he had disobeyed his father who had always been good to him. His heart was broken, and when he went to say he was sorry, his head was down and he began to cry. The boy then said, "Dad, I am really sorry I broke your clock."

The father reached out with compassion and

hugged this son, but the other boy received the punishment he was warned about.

If earthly parents can tell what is in the hearts of their children, how much more does our Heavenly Father know what is in our hearts when we come to Him for salvation?

It is what is in our hearts when we turn to God for salvation that makes the difference of whether we are truly saved or not.

God demands that we humble ourselves before Him and realize that we have broken His laws and have horribly failed to be as thankful as we should be for the gift of life that He has given to us. He demands that we accept and realize that we deserve the penalty of death because of our sins.

It is only as we first meet these conditions of repentance in our heart and are ready to turn to God seeking His forgiveness that we can be saved.

Our salvation is completed when we turn to God in humble, heartfelt repentance and accept the sacrifice that Jesus made on the cross as an atonement for our sins.

Salvation is a life changing encounter with God. He is ready to meet us when we are ready to come to Him on His terms.

I certainly don't want to make anyone doubt their salvation if it is in place, but I feel strongly that a high percentage of people making up the churches of today seriously need to ask themselves these urgent questions:

(1) Am I really saved?

(2) Can I remember a time in my life when I was overwhelmed with fear and guilt, knowing I was on my way to the place of eternal punishment because of my sins?

(3) Has there been a time when I humbled myself and turned to God with all my heart, repenting of my sins and accepting Jesus and His death on the cross to take away my sins?

(4) Has God changed my life and made me a new person?

(5) Is my life now centered around serving, pleasing, and following God to do the work of helping others find the way of life?

If your answers to these questions are all "yes," then you have every right to be the happiest person on the planet, and I rejoice with you, my brother or sister! But if your answer was "no" to any of the questions, then you seriously need to get real with God. The big clock of time is ticking, and nobody knows exactly how many ticks are left!

It is very important to realize that salvation is not a growth or learning "process" that happens over a period of time. It is a spiritual birth and transformation that only happens with a noticeable encounter with God. If you can't remember a time when you were saved, then you are probably not!

If you can not remember a time in your life when you were overwhelmed with fear and sorrow realizing that you were guilty before God and on your way to the place of eternal punishment, then you have never reached the "place of beginning" to receive real salvation. You <u>must</u> humble yourself and first come to this place!

We often see people shedding tears at various events and in situations throughout life. If there ever is a time that is right to shed tears, then at the very top of the list should be when we approach God for salvation realizing how horribly wrong we have been, how we have miserably failed to be thankful for the great gift of life that He has given to each one of us, and how we have broken His laws and are standing guilty and condemned before Him.

I believe that the Spirit of God is going to touch many people's lives as they read this book. If you feel that your walk with God is not real and you might not have had a real salvation experience, or if you are coming to the Lord for the first time, please understand that God's Spirit is leading you.

Here are seven steps you can follow to receive your salvation.

(1) Humble yourself before the great and mighty God and Creator and allow God to reveal to you the reality that your are standing guilty and con-

demned before Him and that the penalty of death and hell has been placed upon you because of your sins.

(2) Believe that Jesus died on a cross and shed His blood to take the penalty and punishment of your sins upon Himself and that He has made a way for you to be forgiven and set free from the penalty you face.

(3) Turn to God with real repentance in your heart for your sins in a broken and, contrite way.

(4) Confess to God that you realize you have broken His laws, and confess that you are guilty before Him and deserve the punishment you face.

(5) Accept Jesus and the sacrifice He made on the cross for the forgiveness of your sins by saying something like: "Jesus I accept you as my Savior and I accept your blood that was shed on the cross as a sacrifice to take away my sins."

(6) Ask Jesus to come into your heart and life. Ask Him to change you and give you the strength to follow Him and be what He wants you to be.

(7) Put your faith and trust in Jesus knowing that He has succeeded in making a way of forgiveness and a way of life. Trust God's Spirit to lead you and know that He alone is your source of strength and help. The more you seek God, the better and easier your pathway will be. Amen!

If you need further help please feel welcome to contact this ministry.

write to: Flame Ministry
          P.O. Box 2501 #254
          Springfield, MO. 65801

call: 1-800-864-5289

e-mail: FlameMinistry@aol.com

Chapter 3

What Do These Parables Really Mean?

Some of the most important truths in the Bible are contained in the parables of Christ. The infinite wisdom of God is revealed in His ability to translate these great truths into simple earthly stories. The only problem is our being able to understand what is meant by these great teachings.

Jesus explained the meaning of some of His parables more than others, but the truth is that the Holy Spirit reveals the hidden truths of these stories to whom He chooses. Matthew 11:25 tells us, *"At that time Jesus said, "I praise you, Father, Lord of heaven and earth, because you have hidden these things from the wise and learned and revealed them to little children."*

The meaning of these parables of Christ, which are some of the most important teachings in the Bible, is not being presented to the modern day church for several reasons:

(1) One reason is that many leaders in the church do not understand the meaning of the parables themselves. Just because a person has a degree, even a Ph.D., does not mean that God has chosen to reveal great spiritual truths to that person. As a matter of fact, according to what Jesus said in Matthew 11:25, God chooses to hide the most important spiritual truths from those who think they are wise and learned. Many leaders who have their degrees and think they have "arrived" might do well in a Bible trivia contest, but actually do not possess an understanding of the most important and vital spiritual truths.

(2) The truth in the parables offends those who are not successfully following and doing what Jesus has commanded all of us to do, especially in the area of taking the message of salvation to others. Unfortunately, the church is mostly filled with people who are failing in this area. Because of being concerned about the success of their church or ministry, most leaders are not willing to present spiritual truths that offend people. The church urgently needs to understand the meaning of these great teachings of Christ because Jesus is revealing how the Kingdom of God really works.

Parable Of Talents

Matthew 25:14-30: *"Again, it will be like a man going on a journey, who called his servants and entrusted his property to them. To one he gave five talents of money, to another two talents and to another one talent, each according to his ability. Then he went on his journey. The man who had received the five talents went at once and put his money to work and gained five more. So also, the one with the two talents gained two more. But the man who had received the one talent went off, dug a hole in the ground and hid his master's money. After a long time the master of those servants returned and settled accounts with them. The man who had received the five talents brought the other five. 'Master,' he said, 'you entrusted me with five talents. See, I have gained five more.' His master replied, 'Well done good and faithful servant! You have been faithful with a few things; I will put you in charge of many things. Come and share your master's happiness! The man with the two talents also came. 'Master,' he said, 'you entrusted me with two talents; see, I have gained two more.' His master replied, 'Well done good and faithful servant! You have been faithful with a few things; I will put you in charge of many things. Come and share your master's happiness!' Then the man who had received the one talent came. 'Master,' he said, 'I knew that you are a hard man, harvesting where you have not sown and gathering where you have not scattered seed. So I was afraid and went out and hid your talent in the ground. See, here is what belongs to you.' His master replied, 'You wicked, lazy servant! So you knew that I harvest where I have not sown and gather where I have not scattered seed? Well then, you should have put my money on deposit with the bankers, so that when I returned I would have received it back with interest. Take the talent from him and give it to the one who has the ten talents. For everyone who has will be given more and he will have an abundance. Whoever does not have, even what he has will be taken from him. And throw that worthless servant outside, into the darkness, where there will be weeping and gnashing of teeth."*

Everything in the parables of Christ represents something in the Kingdom of God. The master in this parable who gave his servants money, went on a journey, and then returned, represents Jesus. The servants in this story represent those of us who profess to be servants of Christ.

In this parable, the master gave his servants sums of money (talents). These talents represent the most important thing Jesus has given to his servants — the message of salvation. The servant who went and hid his master's money and did nothing with it represents those of us who do not share the message of salvation with others and help them come to Christ. The servant who produced no gain with what he had been given received a severe punishment and was "cast out into darkness where there was weeping and gnashing of teeth," which is a phrase Jesus often used when speaking of the place of eternal punishment. Unfortunately, a large percentage of churchgoers fall into the category this worthless servant represents. They have not used the message of Jesus to help even one person into the Kingdom of God.

We cannot earn salvation by working to share the Gospel, but those who have no action in their life of sharing the urgent message of life with others need to realize that their faith is not real. They do not care enough about God in their hearts to do what He has asked us all to do. Jesus is showing us in this parable the great importance of using the most important thing He has given to us — the message of salvation — to help others find the way to life.

The phrase "come and share your master's happiness" portrays Jesus welcoming His good servants into the Kingdom of God. The phrase "and throw that worthless servant outside, into the darkness, where there will be weeping and gnashing of teeth" previews Jesus casting worthless servants into the place of punishment.

Through this parable, Jesus reveals that those who do not obey His command to share the message of salvation with others will not be included in the Kingdom of God, but will be cast out.

Many preachers today are teaching the opposite of what Jesus taught in this parable. They are mistakenly teaching their people that God is not requiring everyone to share the message of salvation with others. They are falsely telling them that He only calls certain people to do this and gives them special gifts to do it. They are helping their people fail in the most important area of following God.

I am sure some of these preachers would like to think the talents in this parable represent something other than the message of salvation. But I would say it is extremely important to keep in mind how severe the punishment was that was dealt out to the worthless servant who failed to use what he had been given. Being thrown out into the darkness where there is weeping and gnashing of teeth is not exactly a little slap on the wrist! The severity of the punishment the worthless servant received should convince everyone that whatever the talents represent must be extremely important. Is there anything more important that God has given to His servants than the understanding of the way of salvation?

If you find you are like this last servant and have not shared the message of salvation and helped others come to Jesus, then you need to either rearrange the priorities in your life so God and His work are first, or you need to turn to God in a way that produces a real salvation experience.

One thing is for certain: no one can earn salvation by doing works. All of our works in the Kingdom of God must be done from a heart that loves God and wants to please Him. If you find that the works are not there, then it's because a right heart is not there. Real salvation produces a "right heart."

Parable Of The Ten Virgins

"At that time the kingdom of heaven will be like ten virgins who took their lamps and went out to meet the bridegroom. Five of them were foolish and five were wise. The foolish ones took their lamps but did not take any oil with them. The wise, however, took oil in jars along with their lamps. The bridegroom was a long time in coming, and they all became drowsy and fell asleep. At midnight the cry rang out: 'Here's the bridegroom! Come out to meet him!' Then all the virgins woke up and trimmed their lamps. The foolish ones said to the wise, 'Give us some of your oil; our lamps are going out.' 'No,' they replied, 'there may not be enough for both us and you. Instead, go to those who sell oil and buy some for yourselves.' But while they were on their way to buy the oil, the bridegroom arrived. The virgins who were ready went in with him to the wedding banquet. And the door was shut. Later the others also came. 'Sir! Sir!' they said. 'Open the door for us!' But he replied, 'I tell you the truth, I don't know you.'" (Matthew 5:1-12)

In this parable, Jesus is obviously the bridegroom. The five wise virgins represent the people who get to go with Jesus when He returns, and the five foolish virgins are those who will not go. One important question, however, is who do all ten virgins represent?

Most people have falsely been led to believe that the five wise virgins represent the church and the five foolish virgins represent the lost world. However, in this parable, all ten virgins knew that the bridegroom was coming and they were all expecting to go with Him. Those who are lost in the world are certainly not expecting Jesus to come and are not expecting to go with Him. Therefore, they cannot be the foolish virgins!

The ten virgins are the crowd of people who are all expecting to go with Jesus — the church crowd. Jesus is warning us in this parable that many of the people who are fully expecting to go with Him when He returns will be left out because they are unprepared.

Isn't it a scary thought that half of the church crowd who all think they are going with Jesus when He comes will be left behind — like half of the virgins who got left behind? I hope it's scary enough to get you to stop and ask yourself some serious questions like: "Am I really saved? Am I really following God? Am I really ready to go?"

I think it is important to notice that it would have been hard to tell the difference between the five wise and the five foolish virgins just by looking at them. Even their lamps looked the same on the outside. It's kind of that way with people, too. Everyone in the church seems to be a Christian on the outside. However, what is really important and what is going to make the difference between who will go with Jesus and who will not is what is on the inside.

Some people have the Holy Spirit on the inside and some do not. Some people have truly been saved in their hearts and have been born of the Spirit of God, and some are just practicing religion. Keep in mind that the Holy Spirit is represented throughout the Bible by oil, and in this parable, it is the oil that made the difference in who was prepared and who was not.

Let us seek Him!

Parable Of The Sower

"A farmer went out to sow his seed. As he was scattering the seed, some fell along the path and the birds came and ate it up. Some fell on rocky places, where it did not have much soil. It sprang up quickly, because the soil was shallow. But when the sun came up, the plants were scorched and they withered because they had no root. Other seed fell among thorns, which grew up and choked the plants. Still other seed fell on good soil, where it produced a crop—a hundred, sixty or thirty times what was sown." (Matthew 13:3-8)

Jesus interpreted the meaning of this parable

in Matthew 13:19-23 when He said, *"When anyone hears the message about the kingdom and does not understand it, the evil one comes and snatches away what was sown in his heart. This is the seed sown along the path. The one who received the seed that fell on rocky places is the man who hears the word and at once receives it with joy. But since he has no root, he lasts only a short time. When trouble or persecution comes because of the word, he quickly falls away. The one who received the seed that fell among the thorns is the man who hears the word, but the worries of this life and the deceitfulness of wealth choke it, making it unfruitful. But the one who received the seed that fell on good soil is the man who hears the word and understands it. He produces a crop, yielding a hundred, sixty or thirty times what was sown."*

This parable is one of the most powerful and important teachings in the whole Bible. In this short story, Jesus explained how all people who hear the message of the Kingdom of God end up in one of four categories.

There are people attending church every week who hear the message of salvation for the first time along with many who have heard the message many times, but do not understand or absorb what they hear. The truth of God seems to flow by these people like water running off a duck's back. They hear the message of Jesus and instead of realizing it is the most important thing in the whole world, the people lose the message in the shuffle of whatever else is on their mind at the time. These people are like the seed that fell along the path that the birds came and ate it up.

There are others in church who are like the seeds that fell on rocky places. They have received the Gospel but are weak and will fall away when trouble or persecution comes like many who have come and gone before.

Then there is a large portion of the church that consists of people who are like the seeds that fell among the thorns. They have allowed the cares of this life to consume their desires and interests to such a point that they have failed to do God's work and are unfruitful. These people exist as church members, just like the plants existed among the thorns, but all their time is spent on the things of this world. They do not take the time to share the message of the Kingdom with others, so they have produced no fruit of leading others to Christ.

But then there are those in the church who are like the seeds that fell on the "good soil." They produce a crop! They make God and the work of His Kingdom everything in their lives and therefore bring forth much fruit. They share the message of Jesus and produce a crop of what was sown in their lives.

Some people believe the crop Jesus was referring to in this parable is something other than spreading the message of the Kingdom of God and helping others find and receive salvation. They choose to believe this way so they won't feel bad about their own failure to bear fruit in the area of spreading the Gospel and winning others to Christ. However, when He says in Matthew 13:23, *"He produces a crop, yielding a hundred, sixty or thirty times what was sown,"* Jesus makes it quite clear that the crop that was produced was a multiplication of what was sown.

In Matthew 13:19, Jesus also tells us plainly that the seed that was sown is the message about the Kingdom when He says, *"When anyone hears the message about the kingdom and does not understand it, the evil one comes and snatches away what was sown in his heart. This is the seed sown along the path."*

This should make it obvious that the crop Jesus was referring to in this parable is a multiplication of what was sown — the message about the Kingdom.

The crop Jesus spoke of in this parable is the souls that are saved when we are obedient to God and share the message of the Kingdom with others. There are things that happen in nature that can hinder fruit being produced, so Jesus used this earthly example to help us see that there are also things in our hearts and lives that can hinder us from successfully spreading the message of the Kingdom and bearing fruit.

Jesus is teaching in this parable that many people who hear the Gospel and perhaps even receive it end in failure. All people who have heard the message about the Kingdom of God are in one of these four groups described in the Parable of the Sower. Three groups failed and one succeeded. Which group are you in?

The Hidden Treasure

"The Kingdom of Heaven is like treasure hidden in a field. When a man found it, he hid it again and then in his joy went and sold all he had and bought that field." (Matthew 13:44)

Through this parable Jesus is revealing that people who truly enter into the Kingdom of God become like the man in this parable who made what he had found more important than everything else in the world.

The man in the parable sold everything and focused all he had on one thing. This is the way our attitude should be if our heart is right toward God. However, the sad truth is many church-going people do not have hearts like this. Many are so engrossed in the things of this life, they just don't have time left for God or His work. Jesus is saying that people who really get saved have a heart toward God and the work of God such as the man in the parable had toward the treasure.

In all the parables discussed in this chapter,

leading others to salvation is a critical element. In no way am I saying a person can be saved by doing the work of sharing the Gospel. But I am saying that when people are truly saved, they will have a heart that has been touched and changed by God, a heart that will produce the work of leading others to Christ. If the works are not there, then the heart may never have been touched and made right, which means that a real salvation experience might not have happened yet. Those who are not strangers to God know that God's spirit of love always leads His people to do the urgent work of sharing the message of Jesus with the lost and perishing people in the world. If you're not doing this, then you are not following the Spirit of God, and you should seriously question why you are not successfully following God.

I would advise everyone in the churches of today to listen to what Jesus is saying through all of His teachings and beware of being misguided by those who preach the opposite of what Jesus taught. Many church leaders are helping people to be unprepared when Jesus returns by preaching that it is not a requirement to share the Gospel and win the lost. Having no works and bearing no fruit certainly did not work for the unfaithful servant in the parable of talents who was thrown into darkness where there was weeping and gnashing of teeth. Jesus did not preach an easy-way Gospel! Christ said, *"But small is the gate and narrow is the road that leads to life and only few will find it"* (Matthew 7:14).

Many leaders in the churches of today are falsely teaching their people by saying that God only appoints some people to share the Gospel and it is all right for everyone else to be a witness for Christ only with their lifestyle. This is a very popular teaching since so many people in the church have zero success in the area of leading others to Christ. However, it is a very wrong and dangerous teaching. Following now is what I believe could be thought of as a "parable" provided by God to depict how ridiculous this false teaching really is.

Different Strokes / Different Folks

As three people walked along a beach, they stopped at a life-guard stand where no life-guard was on duty. Hanging on the stand was the usual life-guard ring with a rope attached. On the back of the stand was a rack that contained several brochures.

As the three people were examining one of the brochures which contained information about how to swim in the ocean, they heard a frantic cry for help and saw a person drowning only a few yards from shore. At this point, all three people wanted to help rescue the person, but each one thought of a different way to do it.

The first person said, "Let's jump in the water, swim out, and try to rescue him."

The second person said, "Let's take the lifeguard ring with the rope attached and toss the ring out to him, and then pull him to shore."

The third person said, "Let's take several of the brochures containing information on how to swim in the ocean, and throw them into the water. Maybe one of them will float out to where he is and maybe he can manage to read the brochure and learn how to swim so he can save himself."

Many people in the church are trying to help others come to Christ only by being a good example and living a good life-style. That is like the ridiculous idea of throwing the brochures in the water. Those who are obedient to God's command and care enough to speak the truth of the Gospel to others are like the good ideas of jumping in the water or throwing the life ring out. Their actions makes sense compared to the urgent need of those who are lost and perishing.

The purpose of my heart in sharing the real meanings of these important teachings of Christ is that it might serve as a "wake-up" call. Hopefully it will help some of the people in the churches of today pull their heads out of the sand, stop being brainwashed by all the ear-tickling preaching and compare themselves to the picture Jesus painted of those who are successful in His teachings.

If your life doesn't match the picture of those who succeeded in these parables, you need to turn to God in a way that produces real salvation and creates within you a "right heart" that moves you to do what Christ has commanded all of us to do.

Then you'll be like the faithful servants in the Parable of the Talents who increased what had been given to them. You'll be like the wise virgins who were found prepared in the Parable of the Ten Virgins. You'll be like the people who were like the seed that fell on "good soil" in the Parable of the Sower who brought forth a crop. And you will be like the man who found the treasure in the field and put aside everything in his life to focus on the treasure he found.

Chapter 4

Observations

I believe that God has given me a very great privilege by revealing some awesome observations concerning His Creation. My faith has been greatly strengthened by what the Lord has enabled me to see. It is my hope and prayer that these observations might increase your faith and maybe even be useful for you to use as tools to witness to the lost.

The Fire Of God

On one occasion, as I was reading through the Bible, I began to notice that along with many of the great miracles God has performed, and as a part of His awesome presence and glory, there was a great manifestation of "fire." Here are some examples of this observation:

Genesis 19:24: *"Then the Lord rained down burning sulfur on Sodom and Gomorra from the Lord out of the heavens."*

God appeared to Moses in a burning bush, Exodus 3:2: *"There the angel of the Lord appeared to him in flames of fire from within a bush. Moses saw that though the bush was on fire it did not burn up."*

God sent hail mingled with fire against the Egyptians, Exodus 9:23-24: *"And Moses stretched forth his rod toward heaven: and the Lord sent thunder and hail, and the fire ran along upon the ground; and the Lord rained hail upon the land of Egypt. So there was hail, and fire mingled with the hail, very grievous, such as there was none like it in all the land of Egypt since it became a nation."*

The Lord guided the Israelites with a pillar of fire, Exodus 13:21: *"By day the Lord went ahead of them in a pillar of cloud to guide them on their way and by night in a pillar of fire to give them light, so that they could travel by day or night."*

The Lord descended on Mount Sinai in a great fire when giving The Ten Commandments, Exodus 19:18: *"Mount Sinai was covered with smoke, be-*

cause the Lord descended on it in fire." Exodus 24:17: *"To the Israelites the glory of the Lord looked like a consuming fire on top of the mountain."*

Exodus 40:38: *"So the cloud of the Lord was over the tabernacle by day, and fire was in the cloud by night, in the sight of all the House of Israel during all their travels."*

The sons of Aaron were destroyed by fire, Leviticus 10:1-2: *"Aaron's sons Nadab and Abihu took their censers, put fire in them and added incense; and they offered unauthorized fire before the Lord, contrary to His command. So fire came out from the presence of the Lord and consumed them, and they died before the Lord."*

Deuteronomy 4:24: *"For the Lord your God is a consuming fire, a jealous God."*

Gideon's offering was consumed by fire, Judges 6:21: *"With the tip of the staff that was in his hand, the angel of the Lord touched the meat and the unleavened bread. Fire flared from the rock, consuming the meat and the bread."*

Numbers 21:6: *"And the Lord sent fiery serpents among the people, and they bit the people; and much people of Israel died."*

When Elijah contested the prophets of Baal on

Mount Carmel, he requested that the real god answer by fire. Elijah allowed them to call on their false god all day long, but they received no response. Then Elijah called on the God of Israel. The Lord God answered by fire with a punctuation mark at the end! 1 Kings 18:38: *"Then the fire of the Lord fell and burned up the sacrifice, the wood, the stones and the soil, and also licked up the water in the trench."*

When Ahaziah sent men to make demands upon Elijah the Prophet, things didn't go so well for the men! 2 Kings 1:10: *"Elijah answered the captain, 'If I am a man of God, may fire come down from heaven and consume you and your fifty men!' Then fire fell from heaven and consumed the captain and his men."*

Elijah was taken to Heaven in a chariot of fire drawn by horses of fire, 2 Kings 2:11: *"As they were walking along and talking together, suddenly a chariot of fire and horses of fire appeared and separated the two of them, and Elijah went up to heaven in a whirlwind."*

In Chapter 1 of the book of the Prophet Ezekiel, we read how Ezekiel received a great vision of the glory of God. First, in verse 4, he saw a great cloud filled with intense fire. Then, in verse 13, Ezekiel described four living creatures, *"The appearance of the living creatures was like burning coals of fire or like torches. Fire moved back and forth among the creatures; it was bright, and lightning flashed out of it."* In verses 26 and 27, Ezekiel saw a vision of God Himself: *"Above the expanse over their heads was what looked like a throne of sapphire, and high above on the throne was a figure like that of a man. I saw that from what appeared to be his waist up He looked like glowing metal, as if full of fire, and that from there down He looked like fire; and brilliant light surrounded Him."*

John the Baptist said that Jesus would baptize us in the Holy Ghost and "fire."

When the power of God came on the day of Pentecost, there appeared tongues of "fire" above the heads of those present.

I was amazed to realize that through all of these manifestations of the glory of God, a great and awesome "fire" accompanied the presence of God and the working of His great power!

As I was thinking about all of this, God said, "Lay your hand upon your body." So I laid my right hand upon my left arm, then upon my neck, and then my face. Then God said, "It's warm, isn't it? It is warm because My fire is in your body. The life that is in you comes from Me and My fire is in you. That is why your body is warm and gives off heat."

At that point, my thoughts were directed to what the Bible says about how God created Adam, how He made Adam's body from the dust of the ground and then breathed into his nostrils "the breath of life." Suddenly I was able to see something so exciting! I was able to see that the breath of life that God breathed into Adam (and that same breath of life that is in each one of us) is the breath of God's FIRE!

My mind went back to some of the basics I had learned in biology, chemistry, and physics classes about the workings of the human body. I remembered that the food we eat is combined with oxygen that we take in through our lungs and is oxidized or "burned." We call a measure of that "burning" a calorie. When God breathed into Adam the breath of life, the fire was started which continues to burn in all of us. When we die, our body grows cold because the fire goes back to where it came from — into the hands of God!

God's fire is different from any fire we know of in this world. God's fire never goes out, it is "eternal." I believe our spirit and soul, comes from the breath of God's "eternal fire" which is the "breath of life" that God has placed in man. It is this "Fire of God" within us that keeps the "burning" process of life continuing as long as we live.

I then remembered reading how scientists were so astonished when they first split an atom. I recalled that they were dumbfounded at the great amount of "heat" energy released from splitting such a small particle.

Today, nuclear power plants that supply energy to huge cities are run by the heat energy released from splitting the atoms of an amazingly small amount of elements. Uranium or plutonium are usually used in most nuclear reactors and bombs because their atoms are easier to split. But if you split the atoms of rocks or other elements, you would get the same results — an enormous release of heat energy or "fire."

Could it be that the "Fire of God" is the power that holds everything together? Just imagine God creating the universe by taking His great power of fire and compressing it down into small particles we call atoms — and when we split these particles, we get a tremendous explosion of God's powerful "fire!"

Science Proves The Bible

For one other amazing thing that I believe God has helped me to see, I would have to give at least some credit to "shopping."

I never dreamed that anything good could ever come from shopping, but with God all things are possible! I guess I'm like most men and just don't "do" shopping very well. I have found that it is a lot less painful for Pam and me if I don't tag along when she is doing the shopping thing. She says it bugs her when I stand outside the store and wait until she is ready to go to the next store because it makes her feel like she needs to hurry or something. I have tried to explain that it really doesn't matter to me which store I am standing in front of waiting, but in order not to cramp her style, I once decided to spend the time in a book store and let her go do her thing. I was interested in looking at some world history books to see how they compared to the Bible. I figure I must have gone into a partial coma when we were studying this stuff in school, but I do vaguely remember studying about Mesopotamia.

It seems like all the world history books agree that the first known civilization of mankind is found in Mesopotamia. Mesopotamia is the fertile land between the Tigris and the Euphrates rivers as they run together before they empty into the Persian Gulf (This area is located in modern day Iraq). When I recognized the location of Mesopotamia, I then realized that according to the Bible, this is also where the Garden of Eden was located!

In Genesis 2:10 the Bible says, *"A river watering the garden flowed from Eden; from there it was separated into four headwaters."* And in verse 14 it says, *"The name of the third river is the Tigris; it runs along the east side of Asshur. And the fourth river is the Euphrates."*

I still wonder if the people who wrote all of

these world history books and the scientists who have made these discoveries realize that their findings provide a tremendous proof of what the Bible says in regard to the Garden of Eden and its location. They have simply discovered the home of Adam and Eve and their descendants, which certainly was the first known civilization of man!

One of the oldest cities that scientists have located in Mesopotamia is the city of Ur. In Genesis 11:31 we read how Abraham was from the city of Ur, *"and together they set out from Ur of the Chaldeans to go to Canaan."* The city of Ur is located very close to where the Tigris and Euphrates run together which is given in the Bible as the location of the Garden of Eden. According to archaeological findings, the city of Ur that Abraham lived in is built on top of an older city that was covered by a gigantic flood!

There is no room for mistake or coincidence here. The Garden of Eden was located in Mesopotamia, exactly where scientists have discovered the first known civilization of man to be. I love it when science proves that the Bible is real. And I praise God even for shopping!

History Proves God

A few years ago there was a lot of excitement about the possible discovery of Noah's Ark. I remember seeing some books about this and watching a TV documentary program on expeditions and searches for the Ark. It was thought that the Ark had been spotted by a plane and had somehow been preserved through all these years. I remember hearing one man say, "Well, if they find Noah's Ark, I'm gonna start believing in the Bible!"

I think there are a lot of people who think the same way. If they could see something "real" existing in the world today that the Bible says happened, then they would believe. Having felt the same way back when I first began searching for the truth, I would like to show you something very "big" that is real in the world today — something that the Bible says actually happened.

God made some tremendous promises one day to a man named Abraham. Abraham and his wife Sarah did not have any children and they were both far past the age of having children. But God spoke to Abraham and promised him that his descendants would be as numerous as the stars in the sky. He told Abraham to leave his home and his family and God brought Abraham into a new land that He promised him and his descendants for an everlasting possession. *"All the land that you see I will give to you and your offspring forever."* (Genesis 13:15)

God even told Abraham how his descendants would be held in a land where they would be strangers for 400 years, but then be brought into the land that God promised to Abraham. It still thrills me to realize that all of this was the beginning of the nation of Israel which has its place in the world today!

The nation gets its name from Abraham's grandson to whom God gave the name "Israel." God did so many great miracles and great things fulfilling all the promises He made to Abraham and establishing the nation of Israel that it spans from the first book of the Bible beginning in chapter 12 of Genesis through the remainder of the whole Old Testament!

Creating the nation of Israel is one of the most important things that God has done in all of creation. It all started almost 4000 years ago with Abraham — and it's still happening at this very moment!

God has promised to give the land of Israel to Abraham and his descendants "forever." To understand this amazing part of God's promise to Abraham, consider the Eternal City of God referred to in Revelation 21:2 *"I saw the Holy City, the new Jerusalem, coming down out of heaven from God, prepared as a bride beautifully dressed for her husband."*

The "New Jerusalem" will be located where Jerusalem is now, which is in the land of Israel that God has promised to Abraham. The names of the twelve tribes of Israel will be written on the twelve gates of this city according to Revelation 21:12, *"It had a great, high wall with twelve gates, and with twelve angels at the gates. On the gates were written the names of the twelve tribes of Israel."*

If you are looking for proof that God is real and the Bible is true, research the history of the nation of Israel. Read about the great promises God made to Abraham to bring this nation into existence, and read about how God has worked in such great ways to bring to pass all that He has spoken to Abraham. Then realize that the people of the nation of Israel in the world today are the descendants of Abraham and they are possessing the land that God promised to them about 4000 years ago. God has fulfilled all of His promises to Abraham and He will fulfill His promises to all of His children throughout eternity!

As God has been faithful to keep His promise and bring the descendants of Abraham into their "promised land," He will be faithful to bring all of His children into the "Eternal Promised Land" as He has promised!!!!!!!

Chapter 5

Golden Calves

In Exodus 32:1-6 the Bible says: *"When the people saw that Moses was so long in coming down from the mountain, they gathered around Aaron and said, 'Come, make us gods who will go before us. As for this fellow, Moses, who brought us up out of Egypt, we don't know what has happened to him.'*

Aaron answered them, 'Take off the gold earrings that your wives, your sons, and your daughters are wearing and bring them to me.' So all the people took off their earrings and brought them to Aaron. He took what they handed him and made it into an idol cast in the shape of a calf, fashioning it with a tool. Then they said, 'These are your gods, O Israel, who brought you up out of Egypt.'

When Aaron saw this, he built an altar in

front of the calf and announced, 'Tomorrow there will be a festival to the Lord.' So the next day the people rose early and sacrificed burnt offerings and presented fellowship offerings. Afterward, they sat down to eat and drink and got up to indulge in revelry."

When Moses had been gone for a long time and the children of Israel could no longer see God doing things among them, they made a serious mistake — one that almost caused them to be wiped off the face of the earth! When the people could no longer sense God's presence, they decided to make a substitute for God. Out of their foolish imaginations, they created a golden calf and called it their god.

I believe the same thing is happening today in many church services and ministries. It is just happening in a different way. I believe many preachers have built "golden calf" ministries.

The church knows that God's presence and glory should be felt in their gatherings before the Lord. However, God's presence and glory has withdrawn from many gatherings because the leaders are more concerned about the growth of their church, ministry, money, or position than they are about following the direction of God's Spirit and doing things His way. They avoid leading people to the unpleasant and fearful place of realizing they are guilty before God and condemned to a place of eternal punishment. A great problem has come from the fact that if we don't flow with God and do things His way, then we flow completely without God. This has brought many churches and ministries to the same place Aaron and the children of Israel arrived at, and unfortunately, they have done the same thing. They have created a "golden calf."

Following now is a parade of Golden Calves:

Golden Calf # 1

God is commonly expected to reveal His presence more in "spirit filled" churches because these people believe they are filled with the Spirit of God and in the gifts of the Spirit. When God's presence fails to appear, people often take matters into their own hands and do ridiculous things — like push people down to the floor and pretend that God is doing it!

There have been times when the glory of God was so strong that people couldn't stand in His presence — like when Solomon dedicated the temple to the Lord. But this is a far cry from watching some preachers today practically break people's necks trying to force them to flop down on the floor! If God decides to make someone fall to the floor, He certainly doesn't need any "neck-bending" help from man.

If people experience the power of God powerfully enough to make them fall to the floor, surely their lives will be changed. However, the embarrassing truth is that the lives of many people who seem to play this "religious game" by falling on the floor every time they get prayed for, never change. Although they claim to be experiencing a great presence and power from God, the same sin remains in their lives and they are not any more motivated to serve God or help other people find salvation. Could it be that much of what is going on here is preachers trying to make themselves look good and trying to make it look like God is doing something?

Golden Calf # 2

We're living today in an era where most things are mass-produced. This works great if we are talking about hamburgers, but not when it comes to the things of God. Unfortunately, this mass-production mentality has slipped into the church today. It's sad to think that the church is trying to "mass-produce" everything from miracles to salvation.

There have always been con-men, impostors, and imitators who stage phony "miracles," but this practice has become common in many church services today. For years we have watched preachers on TV claim miracles are happening when there is no visible proof that anything miraculous has occurred.

The miracles recorded in the Bible made everyone realize God had worked a great miracle. People were filled with awe — and believed in Him. I am convinced that when God works a miracle, He does it in a way that everyone *knows* they've seen one. It brings faith and awareness of God's reality.

Great damage is being done to the work of God by preachers who continually claim that miracles are taking place when there is no evidence of a real miracle happening. The lost people of the world who are watching this religious parade of pretenders are influenced in a negative way. They understandably conclude that God and the whole "religious scene" is a sham.

First Corinthians 12:9-10 lists *"gifts of healing"* and *"miraculous powers"* among the gifts given by the Spirit of God. Therefore, healings and miracles are possible and real. But much of what is happening today is more like cheap carnival theatrics by preachers who operate in their own power and fabricate miracles. If God wants someone to operate in the gift of healing or miracles, He will promote them by actually performing real miracles and healings that leaves people with their mouths hanging open. Unfortunately, most of what we see today is people trying to promote themselves with their mass-produced fake healings and miracles.

Golden Calf # 3

People are chasing back and forth across the country to catch the latest spiritual fad or so-called movement of God. In many spirit filled circles, people's interests are so focused on seeking after signs and wonders and all these so called "manifestations" that it appears they have almost completely forgotten about the urgent work of helping lost people find Jesus. Spirit filled people should be leading the way in the area of helping others find Christ, but according to statistics, they are not. Have they become distracted with "golden calves?"

Regrettably, I have attended several multiple night meetings where the preacher mostly talked about all of these so called "manifestations" of the power of God, and then had people come forward for the grand finale where they ended up flopping on the floor, laughing hysterically, etc.

I know this same thing has been happening all across the country for years. Sadly, I can't even remember the last time I heard a preacher stand up and say something like, "Come, let us pray and seek God diligently to give us strength and power to go and share the message of Jesus to those who are yet lost and dying." This is God's will for all of His people and the direction in which His Spirit is leading. If we follow in the direction of God's Spirit, then His power and presence *will* appear.

The children of Israel did not want to do what was right. They wanted a "Golden Calf," so they got one. The same thing is basically happening today. Most church members do not want to engage in taking the Gospel to the lost, so the preachers find something the people want to hear. Just like Aaron, they give the people what they want — a "Golden Calf."

Golden Calf # 4

There are a lot of preachers in this world who are what the Bible calls "hirelings." They are in it for themselves, not to help others. These preachers find something that is popular and something the people like to hear, and they preach on that. Unfortunately, their teachings usually lead people in the opposite direction that Jesus really wants them to go.

An example of this is all the attention and focus given to "prosperity" during the last several years. People are flocking to hear these preachers who claim to have some spiritual formula for prosperity. They continually lead people to focus and think about what Jesus said for us to *not* think about! In Matthew 6:25 (KJV) Jesus said, *"Therefore I say unto you, take no thought for your life, what ye shall drink; nor yet for your body, what ye shall put on. Is not the life more than meat, and the body than raiment?"* Then in Matthew 6:33 (KJV) He adds, *"But seek ye first the kingdom of God, and His righteousness, and all these things shall be added unto you."*

Jesus is basically saying in these verses that He wants us to focus our thoughts and desires on pleasing God and doing His work, not thinking or worrying about what we have — or don't have!

These so-called "spiritual formulas for prosperity" only work for these hireling preachers when they get people to give them money or buy their tapes or books that somebody needs to take and burn! They distract God's people from focusing on what they really need to focus on — helping others find Jesus.

It's amazing what some of these preachers can get people to believe or do, such as the idea of "giving to get." For example, "You send me money, and God will multiply it back to you." Doesn't this seem sort of like trying to make a slot machine out of God? I really don't think God is going to get very excited about giving anything to someone who is giving with one hand while holding out the other hand to receive more.

Golden Calf # 5

We have other preachers trying to teach us how to claim and confess everything into existence, from possessions to healing. This can seem like a harmless doctrine until we visit the graves of many people, including innocent children, whose lives have been cut short because they did exactly what the preacher taught them. They made the fatal mistake of not seeking medical help for themselves or their children because they were brainwashed by false teaching.

These misguided guides are trying to tell us that Christ has provided perfect health and prosperity for all of us, and all we have to do is just claim it and confess it. Are we really supposed to believe that these modern day "professional" preachers know something that Jesus and the Apostle Paul weren't aware of since neither one of them ever mentioned this idea?

The people who have invented these sound-good doctrines may have been able to make a lot of money selling their tapes and books and preaching their "new-fangled" ideas to gullible people who want to live in religious fairy-tale land. But the blood of many innocent people is upon their hands.

Golden Calf # 6

One of the Ten Commandments is Exodus 20:4, *"You shall not make for yourself an idol in the form of anything in heaven above or on the earth beneath or in the waters below."*

Leviticus 26:1 says, *"Do not make idols or set up an image or a sacred stone for yourselves, and do not place a carved stone in your land to bow down before it. I am the Lord your God."*

In spite of these stern warnings from God, multitudes of people today bow down, kiss, and pray to man-made images of Christian saints and Mary. Yet, 1 Timothy 2:5 tells us: *"For there is one God, and one mediator between God and men, the man Christ Jesus."*

Mary certainly is the most blessed of all women on earth because she had the privilege of bringing the Son of God into this world. But to pray to her or any other saint is only creating an idol no

102

different than the "golden calf." Only God can hear prayers, and praying to anything or anyone else only makes Him angry.

I hope the multitude of people who break God's direct command daily by calling a man "Holy Father" do not think God is impressed with their disobedience. Matthew 23:9 says, *"And do not call anyone on earth 'father,' for you have one Father, and he is in heaven."*

Golden Calf # 7

I have heard it said that what a person thinks about and talks about the most is their God. This makes sense to me because what ever a person thinks and talks about the most is obviously the most important thing to them.

I attended a large gathering of pastors one time and would have to say that if this saying is true, then their God is "numbers." All night long these pastors went on and on about the same thing — how many people attended their church, how many new people had joined their church, and how much their church had grown in numbers.

By the end of the night I was so sick and tired of hearing about "numbers," I felt like standing up and screaming, "Are numbers all you people can think or talk about?" I wanted to say, "Why don't we talk about how many of the people in your church are successful with leading others to Christ."

I think it is time for us to realize that God is

more concerned about "quality" and not "quantity." God is not impressed with our big numbers or our big buildings. It would be wise for church leaders to stop being so totally brain locked on how many more people they can get, and start being concerned about how many of the people they already have are going to be ready when Jesus comes.

Chapter 6

A Time for Revival

If there has ever been a time when the church needs revival, it is now. Webster's dictionary defines revival as: "a bringing or coming back into use or being after a decline; restoration to vigor or activity; a bringing or coming back to life or consciousness."

Truly, as far as the Great Commission is concerned, Christ's Church is suffering a decline, a loss of vigor, even a loss of consciousness. We need to be restored and revived!

We are most certainly living in the last days of this age. The situation this world is facing is critical, and the needs of so many are urgent. Yet great numbers of people in the church are content with merely attending services every week and hearing sermon after sermon, but are never moved to get seriously involved in the urgent work of helping others find the way of salvation.

Many people think their church is having revival if there is a lot of noise and religious hype, or if people are running around wildly or falling on the floor. However, I believe God has His own plan for revival, and the church is not going to see a real revival sent from God until its members start seeking Him and moving in the direction in which His Spirit is leading.

We are not going to see the true power of God demonstrated if we plan to sit around and be entertained, use God's power to help break our attendance records, or any other "self-seeking" desire. The true power of God is sent when His people have an earnest desire for His presence. When they seek His power to share the message of Jesus, the message of hope and life to the lost world, as on the day of Pentecost, then God will send His power. God is not going to send His Spirit until He sees His people seeking Him with a desire to be led and moved by His Spirit to go forth and share the message of salvation with others. I believe He is prepared to pour out His Spirit upon His people in a way that is greater than has ever happened before. But He is waiting for His people to turn their hearts to Him and be willing to follow the leading of His Spirit.

The Bible tells us in I John 4:16, *"God is*

Love." If God's people will turn to Him and seek Him with their whole hearts, He will pour His Spirit of love into their lives, and their hearts will be filled with compassion for the lost. The Bible says Jesus was moved by compassion to minister to people: *"When Jesus landed and saw a large crowd, he had compassion on them and healed their sick"* (Matthew 14:14).

One area of revival we need is to have the love and the presence of God in our lives that is strong enough to move us to action, just like it moved Jesus. However, we are not going to get this kind of revival in some quick and easy way. It's not going to be like getting "fast food" service. The only way we are going to see God move in this great way is when we make up our minds that this is what we want — more than anything else! We must be willing to pray and fast and do whatever it takes to see it happen. It sure is worth whatever it takes to be able to follow the leading of God's Holy Spirit — and experience His power in using us to lead others to Jesus!

Right But Wrong

Suppose one night you wake up and realize your house is on fire. You quickly call 911, and the dispatcher tells you he will send a fire truck right away. Then 30 minutes after you were hoping they would arrive, the truck finally shows up. You are expecting to see everyone jump out of the truck and run to put your fire out. Instead, you are shocked when every "fireman" starts doing things that just don't make sense to you. One starts polishing the truck. Another straightens up the water hose. The Captain starts reading a book, and when you ask him what he is doing, he says he is finishing the Fireman's Handbook of Safety Procedures. He says when he gets the book finished, he thinks it would be a good idea to have an inspection of all of the gear and equipment to make sure it is in top condition.

If you are like most people in a ridiculous situation like that, you would probably "lose your cool" and say something like, "Hey fellows, all this stuff you are doing is really good, but not when my house is burning down — so how about getting a move on it and put my fire out!"

I know this story is pretty farfetched, but aren't many people and churches today being just as ridiculous? They spend so much of their time doing "good things," but leave undone what is most urgent — reaching the lost world with the message of salvation! How much sense does it make for churches to continually engage in various teachings and activities when a majority of their members are failing to do the most important work that Jesus has commanded us to do?

You Can Be Where You Want To Be

Imagine if you can, a field filled with many people and a roaring fire in the middle of it. Because it is very cold, the people who keep close to the fire stay warm and feel good, but the people around the outside who are not close to the fire are freezing and miserable. Those who get really cold and decide to come close to the fire and warm themselves have to stand around the fire for a while before they get warm. As soon as they walk away from the fire, they start getting cold again. Those who stay close to the fire are happy, and those who stay away from the fire feel horrible — some even get sick and die!

In God's Kingdom, there are people who are like those who stay close to the fire. They seek God diligently so they enjoy all the blessings and strength that come from being filled with His Holy Spirit. Then there are those who are like the people who stay far away from the fire. They seldom ever seek God or spend time with Him, so they are weak and miserable. Sometimes we have to spend a good amount of time seeking God before we start feeling His presence, glory, and all of His blessings in our lives, just like those coming in from the cold taking a while to get warm.

An Important Lesson Learned

My wife loves plants, so we have many potted plants on our back deck. Last summer, she went on a trip for several days and put me in charge of watering all the plants while she was gone. I did really well except for a few days. Unfortunately, those few days were all in a row. When I realized I had slipped a little bit, I hurried to the back deck and was mortified to see a "not so pretty sight." One look and I figured all the plants were probably gone. All the leaves were shriveled up and the stems were sagging. There was one plant — the kind that looks like it takes a lot of water — that was completely collapsed. I thought, that puppy is gone for sure! I had a little moment of panic realizing I would never hear the end of this.

But then an idea flashed into my mind. I could fix this situation by going out and buying some identical plants and putting them in the same pots. Maybe my wife would never know.

However, before I put my master plan into action I decided to give the plants a chance for resurrection by drowning them in a lot of water. I thought a few of them might have a chance to revive. When I went to check out the situation only a few hours later, my mouth dropped open. I could hardly believe my eyes! Every single one of the plants had straightened up and looked as healthy as could be. It looked like a miracle. Even the plant that had looked lifeless was standing up and looking great.

A couple of days later, I was feeling frustrated and down because I just didn't feel like I had joy and victory in my life like I knew I should. I had let myself get so busy and had not spent much time with the Lord for a few days. But God is so wonderful and good. He always helps His children get back on His good pathway, even when they wander off.

As I was moping around feeling discouraged, God spoke softly and said, "You are like that plant that was drained and wilted. If you will come to Me, I will drench your soul with My Spirit and you will be like that plant that revived after you poured water on it!"

Why should we walk in weakness when God is always there to help make us strong? Why should we be discouraged and downhearted when God is always there and wants to fill us with joy and gladness? Why should we be defeated when God is always there to lift us up and give us strength to walk in victory?

I am finding that there are two roads in life upon which I can walk. If I spend time with God, He helps me walk on the "High Road," where my life is filled with peace, joy, love, strength, and victory. The more time I spend with God, the higher that road gets. But if I don't spend much time with God, I end up walking on the "Low Road," where my life becomes filled with confusion, weakness, blindness, and discouragement. The less time I spend with God, the lower that road goes. I am going to take the "High Road!" How about you?

If you find yourself "dry" and weak like the plants, remember you can change your situation. Just get alone with God and begin to praise and worship Him — even if you don't feel like it. Keep on spending time with God and see what happens!

Bear in mind that the Spirit of God came upon Samson and gave him the strength of a thousand men. That same Spirit of God can and will change you, if you will diligently seek Him!

Sometimes Doing Nothing Is Wrong

What would you think of a man who came home very late one night and as he pulled into his driveway, he noticed smoke coming out of his neighbors' roof. He realized the neighbors' house was on fire. This man's first thought was to go over and knock on his neighbors' door, but it was very late and he remembered he had to get up early the next morning. So he decided to go on to bed. He thought someone else would see the neighbors' house on fire and warn them, or surely their smoke alarm would go off. But, the next day he learned the neighbors' whole family had died in the fire.

Most people would agree this person was wrong in doing nothing. What he should have done was run over and bang on the door or do whatever he could to warn his neighbors or help save them in some way.

If we who understand that Jesus has made a way for people to be saved from the horrible penalty of death and eternal punishment don't try to help those who are lost, we are just as wrong as the person who did nothing in this story.

Matters Of Urgency

There are several existing conditions that should make us feel an urgency concerning the work of taking the message of salvation to the lost and dying in our world.

First of all, we are certainly living in the last days of this age, a time when Jesus could return at any moment. We can hardly watch a news program on TV or read through a newspaper without being reminded of the signs that Jesus has given us to mark the end of this age. It should be obvious that the world stage is set for a global crisis which will bring the one world government led by the Antichrist into existence, just as the Bible tells us.

Christ said, *"As long as it is day, we must do the work of Him who sent Me. Night is coming, when no one can work."* (John 9:4) This should be a meaningful warning to us today.

Beware of teachers who say Christ could not come today. Their wisdom is not from God, and their words can steal away from your mind and heart the urgency you need. Hide these words of Jesus in your heart: *"No one knows about that day or hour, not even the angels in heaven, nor the Son, but only the Father. Be on guard! Be alert! You do not know when that time will come."* (Mark 13:32-33)

Knowing Jesus can come at any moment and the chances for people to be saved drastically diminish after He comes, we should feel an urgency to help as many people come to Jesus as possible before He returns.

When I was a young boy living on the farm, we used to cut and bail hay in the summer and haul it into the barns. One day as we were hauling in the hay that had been bailed, the sky became dark and the wind started blowing. We knew those were signs that a rainstorm was coming. We started working three times as hard knowing the rain would ruin whatever hay was left in the field. With some hard work, we managed to get all the hay into the barn right before the rain came. Seeing all the signs of Christ's return in the world today should inspire us to work extra hard to help save as many people as we can in the time that is left.

Another thing that should inspire us to hurry along in doing God's work is the fact that people are dying of diseases, accidents, natural disasters, and wars all around us every day. The sad truth is that those who do not repent and turn to God for salvation before they die will never have another chance. We must reach the living with the Gospel before they are gone.

We should also keep in mind the fact that we ourselves are not guaranteed a tomorrow. There are so many illnesses and accidents that can take us out of this life without warning, or put us in a position where what we can do is limited. Therefore, we need to do all we can while we are able.

We need a revival in the area of being aware of these matters of urgency so that it moves us into action and becomes a continuing part of our lives.

As we start seeking God and get busy about His business, it's very important to make up our minds that we are not going to let Satan stop us or distract us. We can be sure he will always try. The devil has a whole sack full of tricks and lies that he will try to get us to fall for.

One of the most successful tactics Satan uses is getting us to take our eyes off of the total victory Jesus won for us on the cross. He wants us to shift our attention to our failures and shortcomings. If our enemy can get us to focus our concentration on our failures and weaknesses, he then magnifies them in our mind. His plan is to make us feel so horrible that we don't consider ourselves worthy to tell others about Jesus — or even be in the presence of God. I think we have all "been there, done that!"

We must keep our mind locked on the fact that Jesus has already won the total victory for us. By His sacrificial death, He has made a way! All of our sins and failures are covered by His blood. We are worthy to be in the presence of God and do His work because Jesus has made us worthy by His sacrifice. If we fail to trust in what Jesus has done and allow the evil forces to make us think our salvation depends upon our performance or works, then we are going to be defeated and feel miserable.

I John 1:9 says, *"If we confess our sins, He is faithful and just and will forgive us our sins and purify us from all unrighteousness."*

If we have been saved by the blood of Jesus which covers all of our sins, and if we have confessed any known sin and have been forgiven according to God's promise, then there is nothing for us to feel guilty about — unless we want to believe a lie from hell.

The Amplified Bible says in Hebrews 10:14, *"For by a single offering He has forever completely cleansed and perfected those who are consecrated and made holy."* This verse gives us a solid platform to stand upon because it tells us that what Jesus did on the cross has completely cleansed and perfected us forever! It is only by realizing that we are made acceptable to God by what Jesus has done and not by our performance that we can walk in victory and freedom.

Another trick Satan uses to try and stop us from working for God is telling us we are going to fail when we share the Gospel with others. But there is no way anyone can fail in sharing the Gospel! Even if we preach the truth and no one accepts Jesus as Savior at that time, we have at least done what God has asked us to do, therefore we have succeeded. There is no failure. There is only success! Moreover, we may not see the seeds of salvation we may have planted that God can continue to water and allow to grow.

We can be set free from the fear of failure in sharing our faith and the message of salvation with others if we can realize it is the Holy Spirit of God who does the work of leading and bringing people to salvation, not our abilities or performance. So if God is the one doing the work, what are we so worried about? He is not looking for people with great ability, just availability.

The most important thing we can do in spreading the good news of salvation is to pray until we feel the leading of God's Spirit — then follow where His Spirit leads. The Bible says God is love so we need to follow where "love" leads us. In other words, pray until we feel concern, love, and compassion for those who are lost. Then follow the direction of what we feel in our heart because that is one of the greatest ways God leads His children.

Remember that faith grows as it is exercised like muscles grow when they are exercised. As we step out and exercise our faith by sharing the message of Jesus with others, we will find that our faith grows stronger and it becomes easier to speak the truth along the way.

Mow The Grass

Suppose one day, before leaving for work, a father gave his son instructions on how to mow the yard that day. The instructions included details such as how to mix the gas for the mower, which direction to mow the yard, where the cord was for the trimmer, etc. Then the father went off to work. However, as he turned into the driveway coming home from work that evening he noticed right away that the yard had not been mowed. As the father entered the house his son came running up to him and throwing his arms around his dad he said, "Dad I think you are so great, I just want to tell you how much I love you." The dad then said, "Well, it's great to hear that you love me son, but if you love me so much then why didn't you mow the yard today like I told you to do?" The boy just kept on holding on to his dad and over and over again telling him how much he loved him until his father finally became disgusted and said, "Why don't you quit telling me how much you love me and go show me that you love me by mowing the grass like I told you to do!"

Every week people gather in the house of God and sing songs of praise and worship to the Lord. They praise God with their lips and some raise their hands. However, a very high percentage of these same people are not making sharing the message of salvation with others the main priority in their lives. Many are not doing anything. Don't you think it's time to "mow the grass?"

Let The Fire Start In Me

As I was driving through a national forest a few years ago, I noticed that a large area had been destroyed by a forest fire. I started wondering what could have started a fire so big and powerful that it destroyed thousands of acres of forest. Then the amazing thought came to my mind that it could have come from something as small as one blade of grass catching on fire. Someone could have flipped a cigarette from a car that landed next to one blade of grass which caught on fire. That blade of grass could have set others on fire around it and in a matter of minutes, there could have been an unstoppable fire raging.

As my mind turned to spiritual matters, it seemed like God used what I had been thinking about to show me something extremely exciting. Any one of us can be like that single blade of grass — God can use any of us to start a great fire of revival.

If we can get focused enough to seek God diligently until we catch on fire spiritually — and make up our minds that we are not going to let anything stop us — the fire in us can spread to others around us and soon there could be a great revival that would just make all the devils have a nervous breakdown!

Just think what could happen if one person became like that single blade of grass and prayed until God breathed the fire of His Holy Spirit into his or her soul. As that person started leading people to Christ, others would realize that they could be doing the same thing. As other people would join in and pray, God would breath His Spirit upon them and more people would get saved. You would have what God considers a real revival! How about you, my brother or sister, being that blade of grass?

Once again, real revival can only come when we follow in the direction in which God's Holy Spirit is leading. God is leading His people to set aside all other cares and turn to Him and seek His Spirit earnestly and diligently. He can then fill our hearts with love and compassion for those in the world who are lost and dying and are headed for eternal punishment.

As God's children turn to Him and are willing to follow His leading and allow the Holy Spirit to move us into action, we will see God do things through our lives greater than we could ever dream. We can experience more love and joy and excitement than we could ever imagine! Those who truly seek and follow the Spirit of God can see their lives change and become more exciting than the greatest of action movies we pay good money to see! Taking the message of life to others and seeing them set free from the penalty of death and hell and receive eternal life is a great privilege for which we should thank and worship God.

The time is now for us to make God everything in our lives, as He deserves to be, and to follow the leading of His Holy Spirit!

Join with me. Let's seek Him and walk with God and see Him bring the greatest revival ever — the end of time revival, the revival in which He will pour out His Spirit greater than ever before! Let it begin now!

Chapter 7

Collectibles

I have this old Bible that my mother brought home one day in a large box of books that she had bought at a garage sale. This was about 24 years ago, and for some strange reason, I took this old tattered Bible and started liking it a lot. I don't really know why because the front and back covers had been torn off and it had been discarded to collect dust in a pile of other books.

I found a piece of leather and made some covers for it, and I have had it ever since. It has larger print and some really cool maps and pictures in it, and through all these years, I have come to treasure my old Bible. It's older than ever and falling apart, but it's just way cool! Sometimes it reminds me of myself because God took my life when it was tattered and ruined and discarded by others, and fixed it up and made something good out of it, just like I fixed up my old Bible.

Many times I get these really great ideas that I believe are inspired from God, and they seem so important that I want to go and write them down so I won't forget them. I have even gotten up in the middle of the night and written some of these thoughts and ideas down in my old Bible. Most of the space in the front and back of my Bible is filled with things I have written through all these years. Sometimes I read through these writings and it seems to encourage and help me, so I would like to share them with you. I hope they will be of some help to you.

There is a very special place of spiritual awareness where victory, love, peace, and joy abound. This is a place where only the Holy Spirit of God can take you. It is a place that cannot be reached by any human effort, but can only be reached as the Spirit of God fills our lives. God has absolutely everything we need — we must just learn to seek and trust Him.

We should spend time with God and worship Him just because we love Him. We should not always be trying to get things from Him. Our Heavenly Father sees all that we need and will give us more than if we had asked.

All the work we do for the Kingdom of God

should be done out of love for God, and for people and their needs, not out of fear of punishment. If we don't love Jesus enough to put aside everything and follow Him, then we just don't love Him enough!

Seek the Lord God, be filled with His Spirit, and walk in the fullness of His Spirit. Faith drives out doubt; love drives out selfishness; peace drives out turmoil; understanding drives out confusion; light drives out darkness; beauty drives out ugliness. Seek the fullness of God's Spirit to abide in your soul and trust in His strength.

If a person does not pray and spend time with God, the light of God's Spirit grows dimmer and dimmer while the darkness of doubt, confusion, and all manner of wrong grows greater. But, praise be to God, when we return and spend time with Him, the strength of His light grows so strong that all the darkness disappears, and the glory and the light of His love abides.

A really cool comparison of how the Spirit of God works in our lives is comparing the power and presence of God's Spirit to that of a "glow in the dark watch." The material on the hands of a glow in the dark watch absorbs energy from sunlight and the hands glow when you enter a dark room. However, the watch must be exposed to the sunlight before it can glow and then it will only glow in the dark for a certain length of time. As it loses the energy that it had absorbed, the glow gets weaker and weaker.

As we spend time in God's presence praying and worshipping the Lord, His Holy Spirit comes into our "inner being" or spirit and brings strength and blessings. God's spirit flows into our life, mixes and mingles with our spirit, and brings faith, love, understanding, power to resist sin, peace, and joy! The longer we spend in God's presence, the more power and strength and blessings increase in our lives. The truth is, however, that just like the glow in the dark watch loses the energy it had absorbed unless it is re-energized, we lose the power and strength that comes from God if we fail to spend time with Him. So, if we are weak and empty, guess who is to blame?

Our faith is strengthened when we pray, read the Bible, listen to inspired teaching or preaching, and exercise our faith by sharing the Gospel with others.

It is very important to help lost people understand that when they get saved, they become a totally new person. They are completely transformed into a new being. It is very hard for some lost people to believe that they can ever follow God and live a good life because they can only see themselves the way they are and not what they can become. Helping them to understand that they can be changed and become a new person empowered by God gives them hope!

God is LOVE. Follow where LOVE leads! Follow your heart, not your head!

Trust in the Holy Spirit to supply power, understanding, and direction when you reach your destination. If you are trying to figure out what you are going to say and do before your get there, where is your trust in God?

The key to having success in our lives (like walking in victory and strength and living an overcoming life) is in having the presence of God's Spirit in our lives. The key to all success in doing the work of God is having the presence and flow of God's Spirit in what we do.

We must be born into the spiritual family of God like we are born of the flesh into our natural family.

God loves His children! He will not kick any of His children out of His family any more than we would kick our children out of our family.

Just as we don't like to abide or live in a sloppy or dirty house, God does not want to dwell in our temple if it is not kept clean from sin and the cares of this world.

Jesus is a wonderful savior. But He can only be a savior to those who are willing to humble themselves and realize that they <u>need</u> a savior.

Don't forget that a great collapse is coming to this world system. You must work hard while you can. Jesus can come any day, and people are dying and destroying their lives all over the world every day.

It would be wrong to be live among people who were starving to death and have a large storehouse of food and not give any of the food to save people's lives. So it is wrong to know the truth of salvation and not share it with others because their needs are truly greater than people starving to death. They face eternal death.

Faith can be like yeast in bread. You can take a little bit of dough that has yeast in it and add it to some fresh dough and soon that dough will be full of yeast. We can take a little bit of our faith, share it with someone else, and soon that person's life can be totally changed and full of faith.

We need to learn to trust God for absolutely everything we need. We can trust God to supply us with all we need to sustain life such as food, clothing, shelter, etc. We can also trust God to give us understanding and direction, faith, love, peace, joy, and strength to overcome all that is wrong and walk in victory — EVERYTHING !!!!!!!

When a bottle is empty, it is full of air. But as you pour water into the bottle, the air is forced out and the water remains. A Christian is like this in that as God fills us with His Spirit, our sins, doubts, cares of this life, selfishness, and bitterness (which are all of this world), are forced out and the spirit of love takes their place.

Refusing the gift that God offers and holding on to the pleasures of sin and the things this world offers is like settling for a few crumbs and scraps out of the garbage in place of a well-prepared meal with all the trimmings.

When you have a problem, the more you look at the problem the larger it gets. Therefore, look to God and the problem will get smaller as He gets bigger!

Feed your faith and your doubts will starve to death!

Prayer is to faith as breath is to life.

You can tell what you have in the Kingdom

of God by what you have been giving away!

No tears = No salvation

Man builds his churches, God builds his Kingdom.

Sin is like a weed that grows up in a garden. When a weed springs up it can seem small and harmless, but if that weed is allowed to grow, it can quickly mature and produce other weeds. If these weeds are allowed to grow, they can soon fill the whole garden with weeds that will choke out the good plants.

Even when the first weed is small, if you only cut it off at the ground, the weed will just grow back. The only way to get rid of that weed is to pull it up, roots and all, and throw it out of the garden. You could also put some weed killer in the garden that would keep the weeds from ever getting started or coming back.

The Holy Spirit can perform like a weed killer in our lives. He can keep sin from ever getting started or coming back if we sincerely seek Him.

An example of how sin can destroy a person's life like weeds can destroy a garden involves a man who is happily married and has a good wife and family who starts having lustful thoughts about another woman. If those thoughts are not cast out, soon the thoughts will increase like weeds growing in a good garden. If the man allows the sin to continue, he could soon end up having an affair that could destroy his family and his whole life — just like a garden where the weeds were allowed to spread until they took over and ruined the garden.

We need to seek God so that His Spirit can act like the "weed killer" and keep thoughts and desires and sin from getting a foothold in our lives. But if we notice a weed growing in our garden, we should pull it up by the roots and throw it out before we end up with a garden full of weeds!

Our Christian lives are like a tin can full of holes that someone has placed water in and is leaking out. Our strength, faith, power, and love leaks out of our lives when we are not seeking the presence of God. But even if a can has holes in it and leaks, one can pour a big bucket of water in it and fill it up until it runs over.

As we seek God to fill our lives with His Holy Spirit, even though His goodness "leaks out" of our lives, we can be filled and become overflowing with His Spirit. We just have to remember that our can does have holes in it. Therefore, we have to keep filling it up, or we could soon find that our can is empty.

There is a story about a little boy who, when he was very small would play a game when he was at his grandfather's house. His grandfather would put a piece of candy in one hand and hold out both of his closed hands. The little boy would touch one of his grandfather's hands and when he guessed which hand the candy was in, he could receive the candy. Every time he visited his grandfather, the little boy would go up and touch his grandfather's hands because he wanted to play that game and get some candy.

When the little boy grew up and went to his grandfather's house, he would still go and touch his grandfather's hands, but for a different reason. It wasn't for the candy. He just loved his grandfather and only wanted to hold his hands.

I'll bet God would like for His children just to come to Him sometimes, not always to get something, but because they love Him and want to be with Him.

On a cloudy, nasty day, we might long for the sun to come out, but there is nothing we can do as humans to control the forces of nature. However, a great wind could blow all of those clouds and bad weather out of the sky, and the sun could come out and make a beautiful day. God is like that wind when our lives are full of confusion and weakness and doubts. We have no power over the evil forces of darkness that constantly try to defeat us any more than we have power to move the dark clouds out of the sky. But God is like the wind, and His powerful spirit can work in great ways to push the forces of darkness out of the way so that the sunshine of His love can turn our dark and gloomy situation into a spiritually bright and glorious day. Let the winds of His Spirit blow in your life!

A young man received a new car from his dad on his 16th birthday. His dad had paid twenty thousand dollars cash for the car. One day, the young man found that he could borrow money by using the car for security, so he borrowed ten thousand dollars against the car. He was supposed to pay the money back in payments, but the young man began to party and spend the money until it was all gone.

One day, a collector came to the dad and said he was going to have to repossess the car because the young man had not made the payments. This made the father very angry and sad, but instead of letting the car be taken, the father paid the debt that was owed.

How do you think the dad would feel if the boy came to him after this happened and with a nonchalant attitude said something like, "Hey dad, sorry for that little trouble with the car... thanks for taking care of that for me. Hey, me and my friends want to go cruising so can I have my car back now?"

Most dads would probably be pretty ticked off if something like that happened and I doubt if many kids would get their car back until they convinced their dads they realized how big of a mistake they had made and showed sincere sorrow about it.

Our Heavenly Father is that way, too. He doesn't pass out real salvation unless people come to

Him with their hearts broken and show some real repentance.

To contact this ministry:

write to:
Flame Ministry
P.O. Box 2501 #254
Springfield, MO. 65801

Telephone:
1-800-864-5289

e-mail:
FlameMinistry@aol.com

NOTES

NOTES

NOTES

NOTES

NOTES

NOTES

NOTES

NOTES

NOTES

NOTES